# ONE SMALL BOY'S LIFE

## A True History

THE MEMOIRS OF DEREK BISHOP

Mereo Books

2nd Floor, 6-8 Dyer Street, Cirencester, Gloucestershire, GL7 2PF
An imprint of Memoirs Books. www.mereobooks.com
and www.memoirsbooks.co.uk

**A True History of One Small Boy's Life**

ISBN: 978-1-86151-351-9

First published in Great Britain in 2021
by Mereo Books, an imprint of Memoirs Books.

Copyright ©2021

The address for Memoirs Books can be
found at www.mereobooks.com

Mereo Books Ltd. Reg. No. 12157152

Typeset in 11/15pt Century Schoolbook
by Wiltshire Associates.
Printed and bound in Great Britain

# Dedication

✧ ⋯ ✧

This book is dedicated to the memory of Sheila, my beloved wife,
my only girlfriend for 54 years, who gave me many years of
happiness and supported most of my unusual ideas during my life.
She passed away on July 27th 2007. Thank you my dear.

*Enjoy Reading*

*Derek Bishop*

# Contents

Acknowledgement

# Acknowledgement

Many thanks to Vanessa Hitchman, who was able to read my writing and put it in book form. I could not have completed this book without her help.

## CHAPTER 1

# The pre-war years

❖—❖

My first recollection of life was standing at the top of the stairs at 22 Woodlands Road in Romford, the house in Essex where I was born. A builder owed my father some money and he purchased this semi-detached three-bedroom house with a garden for £725 in part exchange. I remember I was dressed in a velvet suit, stomping

22 Woodlands Road, Romford, where I was born and later leaded
the number 22 in the door

my feet and shouting. My friend lived in the same road but I did not want to go to his birthday party. My poor Auntie Marie, who was my father's sister, was looking after me as my mother and father ran a glass and leaded windows business at 116 Park Lane in Tottenham.

My father, John Bowlzer, married my mother, Dorothy Fuggle, on 14th September 1929. My father was born in a small terraced house in Plaistow, London, and had three brothers and three sisters. His father, Samuel Bowlzer, worked as a machine driver at Beckton Gas works. Grandma would cook him a huge meal for when he came home, and then he went down the pub on the corner to drink four or five pints. He was never violent, just merry.

I remember when we went to visit my father's father in Plaistow. He lived in a terrace house with the front door opening onto the street outside. The toilet was at the end of the garden and had newspaper cut into squares jammed on to a nail. I used to play in the road with the other children and we would chase the rag and bone man on his horse and cart, when he would be shouting 'Rags and metal scrap wanted.' If we could find any scrap metal, he would give us a goldfish in a bowl which we would gleefully take home.

My father was apprenticed to John Newton & Sons in Shoreditch to learn the art of glazing and leaded windows. He used to tell me that when all the glaziers went on strike, all the apprentices were forced to go out with panes of glass strapped to their backs on wooden frames. The men jeered and threw stones at them, smashing the glass. My father passed his apprenticeship and married my mother in 1929 when she was a waitress at the Lyons Tea House in London.

In 1934, my father changed the family name from Bowlzer to Bishop. My great grandfather was German and in the 1930s anyone with a German-sounding name was looked at with suspicion.

My parents scraped up enough money to start their own business at 116 Park Lane in Tottenham. My parents used to go dancing and my father played the drums in a small band. My mother gave birth to my brother Anthony in June 1936. Anthony was born with kidney disease and spent a lot of time in Great Ormond Street Hospital, London.

Myself and my brother Tony 1938

My mother used to cut up the sheets of glass and taught herself to make leaded windows. My father bought a second-hand 1932 Ford 1-ton van and used to go out to the housing sites fitting the glass. The glass came in wooden glass cases from Belgium, packed with straw and paper, and were stored ten high in the yard behind the shop. I vividly remember when I was about five, going into the yard with a one-penny pack of seeds from Woolworths, to put some flower seeds in the small patch of garden my father had given me. I decided to have a small fire on the path by the side of the small garden. I got hold of a Swan Vesta matchbox, then put the paper and straw on the path and struck a match. The straw and paper ignited immediately, singeing my hair, and somehow the wooden cases caught fire. I ran into the shop screaming. My poor father had to call the fire brigade and it took two hours to control the flames. I got the cane on my legs from my mother for that.

My father's business was doing well, and they moved to larger premises at 110 Park Lane Tottenham. The premises had wooden racks to store the different types of glass. It had a large bench covered with felt and three large benches where the men would be cutting the coloured glass into shapes before making the leaded windows. I was quite fascinated by this, and after they went home I would creep in and stand on a wooden box and put the bits of lead, which were shaped like a tram line, around the pieces of glass I found under the benches. I turned the gas soldering iron on and attempted to make leaded windows. All the men used to smoke, and in the packets of cigarettes were film star cards which they would stick on the wall over their benches. I used to stand on tiptoe on the benches and take the cards. The men went on strike, and I got a good whacking from my mother for that too.

I liked the different colours in glass and the workshop was full of all sorts of pieces which were the offcuts from a large sheet of glass, being 4-8 feet wide and 3-4 feet high. Very often the cases of glass were stacked outside the shop on the pavement (health and safety would have a field day today). On one side of our shop was Mr Glads, the greengrocer, and on the other side was Mr Livermore, the dairy. They had a son, Peter, and we used to go roller skating on the tarmac road leading to the dairy.

There was a tramp who used to shuffle along our road with cardboard pieces on his back, tied with a rope to his waist. He used to pick up all the cigarette ends in the gutter and then roll them in a thin paper and sit on the bench puffing away. Peter and I got some horse manure from the stable where they kept the horses and dried it and rolled it in a cigarette paper and then put it in the gutter. We watched the tramp pick it up, thinking someone had dropped a whole cigarette. He then sat on the bench and tried to smoke it. We curled up with laughter, with tears in our eyes, seeing the expression on his face. Those were the sorts of pranks we got up to in 1938.

My parents were busy trying to expand their business and I made my own amusement. I had pedal bikes, model cars and trains, and when the men went home at 5.30 they often had to scour the street to find me and take me home.

We lived in a flat above the glassworks, with a large room at the front overlooking the road. Opposite us was a pub and my father used to have a drink on Saturdays and play darts. I remember that one week, after my mother and father had paid the men their wages, they had half a crown left and it dropped between the floorboards in the kitchen. They had to cut a hole in the floorboard to recover it so that we had something to eat that weekend.

My parents often used to go dancing in the local dance hall. When father met some of his business contacts, we often had a babysitter as my brother Tony was only about two years old and needed looking after and I used to make her life hell. Needless to say, we had a lot of babysitters. Soon after this, in 1938, my father built a house at 52 Mapleleafe Gardens in Barkingside, Ilford.

Mapleleafe Gardens, the house my father built in 1938 in Barkingside, Ilford

## CHAPTER 2

# A wartime childhood

W hen I was five I went to a junior school in the same street
where we lived, which was nearly opposite Tottenham Hotspur
Football Club. In 1939, war was declared and our school was bombed
and demolished. It was then decided by the authorities that the bombing was getting worse and all the children from junior schools in the
London area should be evacuated to the country.

I was given a gas mask in a box. An identity tag was attached to
my collar, and my mother gave me a suitcase full of new underclothes,
shirts and socks. About a hundred of us gathered at Tottenham Station
and were sent off to Tiptree in Essex. I ended up in a semi-detached
house and there were four of us in one bed. I hated it. We were given
the poorest of food.

After I had been there for three months, my mother and father came
to see how I was getting on. They were horrified to see I had dirty
underclothes and holes in my shoes and nits in my hair. There was a
shouting match between my mother and the people who were supposed to look after us, and they decided to take me back to London.

The bombing of London was continuous night after night, so

my parents decided to move back to Romford, to the house I was born in, at Woodlands Road. We had an Anderson shelter in the back garden and when the air raid siren started wailing we trooped down to the shelter. After we had done this for a couple of weeks my parents decided that if we were going to die we might as well die in our own beds. One night a bomb exploded very close, and all our lovely leaded windows that my father had made were blown out, leaving a tangle of broken glass and lead. A lot of our tiles were also shattered by the bombing. I used to watch from the oriel window in my bedroom, which was in the front of the house. I remember the searchlights criss-crossing the sky, trying to locate the German bombers, and the roar of ack-ack guns as the shells went up in the sky, sometimes hitting a bomber. I listened to the whine of the engines and then heard the loud explosion as it hit the ground.

I went to St. Edwards Junior School in Romford and every morning, with my school friends, we would collect the pieces of shrapnel and incinerated bombs which we would find in the gutters and on the path. St. Edwards School was at the start of the market and we went down a long drive with small terraced houses on the left-hand side. I cannot say I enjoyed school. We often had the cane if we had done wrong, and once I had to stand in the corner with a dunce's hat on. I was a loner and enjoyed coming home. I got my own tea because both of my parents were working. The people in the house at number 24 were the Cobdens who ran two gents' outfitters shops. They had this 'box' delivered in the sitting room on which you could hear and see people moving. It was a television set with a nine-inch picture! All of the neighbours came into watch. By this time most of the houses had lost their windows and were boarded over with a material called 'sisal craft'.

As the war raged on we accepted the bombing as a way of life, but in 1942, Hitler's Germany invented the V1 and V2 rockets, which were bombs which flew pilotless. They made a funny droning noise and when the noise stopped, they would drop and explode, destroying everything in their path. We used to stand outside and watch them drone over. When the engine stopped, we knew we were safe, as they then glided for about two miles before exploding wherever they landed. It would send a shiver through us, but after a while we took it in our stride.

Opposite us was a block of four very nice houses and in one of them lived Mrs Norton, a smart retired school teacher about 70 years old who used to say hello to me and give me sweets or chocolates on the way to school. The walk to school was about three quarters of a mile. One night, the bombing was at a peak and an almighty explosion occurred, shaking our house to pieces. I hid under the covers, and in the morning, when it was light enough, I was filled with horror to see that the four houses opposite had been reduced to a pile of rubble and smoke and flames were shooting up to the sky. The ARP (Air Raid Precautions) were there with the auxiliary fire brigade searching the rubble for survivors. They never found any trace of Mrs Norton, who had been blown to smithereens. The memory of this has remained with me to the present day.

Auntie Grace and Uncle Frank lived in a large house with a billiard room at Bexleyheath in Kent, and they invited our family over for Christmas. When we arrived, the house was freezing because they had no coke for the boiler and we had Christmas dinner with our overcoats on. My mother wore her fur coat. We did not stay for Boxing Day and drove home to our coal fire. Uncle Frank was in the glass business in competition with my father. He was a bit of a rogue! Grace was my father's sister. They had two children: a child called Patsy who thought she was the cat's whiskers, and Ian, who was nearly blind and wore glasses with very thick lenses.

My parents then decided we must move to a safer place. We moved to a small semi-detached bungalow in Essex called 'Greenway' in Great Tarpots, South Benfleet. A ditch full of water ran past the front of the bungalow and it was very damp. This was only temporary while my father looked around to buy a suitable property. They then bought

'Floreat Linden' at Great Tarpots. The house my father bought during the war to escape the bombing

a detached house with an acre of ground called 'Floreat Linden' in London Road, Great Tarpots, about ten miles from Southend-on-Sea. It had gas lighting, with gas mantels. You pulled a small metal chain with a ring on the end and when the gas came out you lit it with a match. It would make a hissing noise, the mantel would go white and you had light. When you went to bed you pulled the chain on the opposite side to cut off the supply of the gas. Our toilet was in a little outhouse attached to the back of the house and our drainage system was a septic tank in the garden, which my father would bail out with a bucket every month and pour over the garden.

We had a coal fire in the lounge but no other heating. In the winter it was so cold that I used to sleep with my socks on and pull the blankets right over my head. In the morning the windows were all frozen over with a pretty pattern of ice, and to see out you tried to scrape the ice with your fingernails. The kitchen had a concrete boiler in the corner and the water had to be boiled, and the washing was scrubbed on a wooden board with square pieces of fairy soap.

The washing was then put through the rollers of the wringer that you had to turn the handle to operate, and finally hung on a rope clothes line to dry.

The stairs were at the back of the house with a door leading to the front sitting room. There was no bathroom, so we had large tin baths which we used in front of the fire in the sitting room. We often had thick slices of bread toasted on a piece of wire and covered in dripping. They were scrumptious. Those were the days! I used to be given two shillings and sixpence wages every week in a brown wage packet, the same as the men my father employed.

The house stood on the main road with a large verge on the outside. A path from the footpath went over a ditch which ran along the front of the houses. This ditch was covered with thick wooden boards, and when the ditch filled after torrential rain the water would flow over the path.

I used to catch a bus to go to school, South Benfleet Elementary School. The fare was threepence return and I sometimes walked home so I could spend the money on sweets. My father, who had two 30 hundredweight Ford lorries, had them both commandeered by the fire service for the war efforts and they paid my father £7 a week, which was ours to live on. My father bought a 1936 Ford car for £20 and cut off the back of it and turned it into a small truck. He then built a wooden frame in the back to carry sheets of glass. My mother bought some chickens and we had an allowance of mash to feed them with. A red powder called Kanwood spice was added to make the hens lay more eggs.

Great Tarpots was a small village on the main road, with the Tarpots public house on the corner, a modern pub built just before the war. There were also about 25 shops, a post office and a magical fish and chip shop. On Saturday I did the shopping. I went with a shopping list to Mrs Clark and to the grocers for the groceries, which would not cost any more than six shillings plus a coupon from our ration books. The water biscuits were about four inches square and hard; today even a dog would turn his nose up at them. I would go to the greengrocer for the potatoes and vegetables, which were weighed on scales (sometimes I got an extra potato) and all put loose into the shopping bag my mother had given me. I would then go to Mr Palmer, the corn chandler, to get the mash for the chickens. Sometimes on Saturdays I would see the farmer in his peaked cap, jacket, leggings, trousers and boots and he would drive up in his 1928 Model T Ford Truck to pick up the sacks of mash and grain. He would then turn the starting handle to start the truck, jump in quick and go jogging up the road at about 35 miles an hour. As a small boy I was always fascinated with the Ford Model T truck and I am happy to say that since 2007, I have owned one.

I used to visit my father's sister Sue and her husband Bert, who lived in a bungalow on an unmade road with ruts in the centre, and had a daughter called Diana. I was not keen on girls, so I never played with her. One Sunday I went round to see them. The bungalow belonged to my Uncle Frank, our rich relation, who let them live there. I saw this white car with a lot of people crowded around it and I could see when I got closer, that it was a white SS Jaguar, which my uncle had managed to buy. He took me for a ride and I thought I was royalty. When I got home I told my father and he said 'Trust Frank to have the best.' My father was a mason and my parents used to go to dinner dances, all dressed up in their best bib and tucker.

We had a D coupon for sweets and I was allowed threepence worth. I used to like the large humbugs and aniseed balls. My parents worked all week in their glass business and at weekends my mother would cook a roast beef dinner on Sunday with suet roly poly for sweet. I could eat anything and I would have second helpings of pudding with lashings of sugar. On Monday we had cold meat with mashed potatoes and pickles with vegetables left over from Sunday, fried in dripping fat. This was called bubble and squeak. The remainder of the suet pudding was fried in the frying pan, and as usual I would have two or three slices with lashings of sugar.

Looking back to when I was young, I see now that I was no angel. My mother used to make three dozen fairy cakes every week and a large fruit cake. When I came in I would sneak three fairy cakes and rearrange the display so she never found out. One day I felt hungry, so I turned the fruit cake upside down and cut a large piece out and put the cake back on the stand. To my horror my mother had invited some friends for tea, shrimps, watercress sandwiches and the fruit cake. You can imagine her face when she cut the cake and there was nothing underneath. The friends had a good laugh, but my mother was furious and when she got hold of me, gave me several whacks of the cane on the backs of my legs. Painful but the cake was nice.

My mother could cook anything. She made jam, bottled fruits for winter, pickled cabbage and onions. I used to answer back to my father and one day I overstepped the mark and he chased me down the garden, threatening all sorts of punishments. Fortunately, I could run faster and climbed up a tree, and as he stood under the tree shaking his fist at me, I spat on his balding head (he had lost most of his hair). I had to stay up the tree until nine o'clock and had to go to bed with nothing to eat or drink. I said sorry the next day. My father, who was quite soft, smiled and said 'don't do it again'.

I worried my father. He lost his hair and spent a fortune on try-ing to get it to grow. Silver green onions, any new concoctions, he would use it. Sometimes I would say to him I could see shoots of hair growing, and looking pleased he would say, 'Do you think so?' and give me half a crown, a new source of income. Looking back, I had an exciting childhood.

I started to do quite well at school, although I hated sports, especially being frozen to death kicking a ball on the field. I was usually a fullback, which was quite boring.

I passed a scholarship at the age of 11 to go to Westcliff-on-Sea High School for Boys. As my parents were not poor, they paid part of my education fees. The lower form was divided into four teams, East, West, North and South. I was in East team, wearing light blue and dark blue horizontal stripes. Our school uniform was a dark blue jacket and caps with badges, grey trousers and black shoes. Caps had to be worn at all times, or you would face two hours' detention on Saturday morning.

I used to catch the bus run by the Benfleet and Canvey Island Bus Corporation, which was owned by Mr Bridges. I had always been interested in growing plants, and I decided to dig some of the garden into small beds, about six feet wide by twenty feet long with grass paths in between. I became the youngest member of the Wartime Allotment Society and I decided I would grow vegetables for the family.

We had a large garden, and one afternoon I decided to clear the lower half, which was covered with brambles and huge clumps of grass. I thought I would burn it off a little at a time, so I put newspaper on the grass and set it alight. After a couple of minutes the flames were roaring and crackling through the garden. I ran back to the house and my father came rushing out with no shoes on and said 'My God, what has he done now!' By this time the fire was out of control and he called the fire brigade. Two fire engines arrived, but in the end I had burned the lower gardens of three other houses. It cleared all the ground and my father apologised to the neighbours. I got someone to plough it up and planted it with potatoes.

My father was conscripted to the AFS, Auxiliary Fire Service, part-time as there was no glass available. His job, with three men, was to board up broken windows in London, and my mother helped him.

We used to hate the Germans, despite some of our relations years before having actually been German. I used to stand outside at night and watch the searchlights. One Sunday they shot down a Dornier bomber and we saw it coming down, smoke and flames bellowing from it. We saw a parachute coming down with a man on it. We young ones chased up the road and the parachute went down at a farm called Sapers Holt. The airman had hanged himself between the power cables. Our group, including myself, danced round underneath shouting 'hooray! Another German bastard dead.'

The Germans discovered there was an oil refinery at Canvey Island close to us and we were in the firing line once again. The Governor of Westcliff-on-Sea High School decided we should be evacuated to a safe area, a place called Belper in Derbyshire, some 350 miles away. I still had unpleasant memories of my previous evacuation.

I remember arriving at Belper Station, where we all assembled on the station platform and various people who were going to accommodate us looked us over. A nice couple in their thirties asked me my name and I followed them into a small saloon car and they drove me to their home about three quarters of a mile from the station. They gave me sausage and mash to eat and a cup of tea. They had one child, a girl, about four years old. I was given a small but nice room and I unpacked my belongings and looked out of the window, which overlooked open farmland.

I went to school the next morning and made a friend by the name of John. After school we used to stand on the railway bridge and take note of all the trains, names and numbers. I cannot remember the name of the people who looked after me, and although they were very nice, I missed my parents and used to cry myself to sleep every night.

At school we had an English master called Mr Midgely, who I hated. My friend and I were convinced that he was a German spy. We used to watch him and noted his movements. Of course he wasn't a spy but we were convinced he was. I was very unhappy and I sent my father a telegram saying 'Bring me home or I am running away.' He promptly came down by train, thanked the people for looking after me, looked at me, and said 'get your things packed.' I had been evacuated just six months.

When I arrived home from Belper to Floreat Linden, my mother said to my father 'What are we going to do with him?' They were both working in the business and there were no schools open locally. It was decided that I could stay at home and look after my brother Tony. I used to clear the ashes from the grate every morning, chop up the firewood and lay the fire ready to light up at about 4 o'clock in the afternoon.

I did all the shopping. My mother gave me a list of groceries to get from Mrs Clark, the grocer in the centre of the parade of shops. Everything was on ration and we had a book of coupons for the purchase of the goods. Everything was in sacks; sugar, tea, flour and rice. Sometimes we had biscuits (only plain ones). which were very crunchy. The greengrocer used to weigh out the potatoes and vegetables and put them into to the shopping bag you took with you. We had a wonderful fish and chip shop, which was open three days a week and I could get a bag of chips with salt and pepper in a greaseproof bag filled to the top for two pence; they were delicious. Sometimes all the family had fish and chips; what a treat!

My brother Tony was not well and my mother had to take him up to Great Ormond Street Hospital in London every month. I did not know at time he had kidney failure and he would eventually die from this disease.

We used to keep chickens and it was my job to feed them and collect the eggs. I also had to clean the chicken house of all the droppings. The house I lived in was one of the 5 detached houses, each having an acre of garden. I decided to dig up some of the garden and plant vegetables. I started to grow potatoes, lettuces, radishes, onions and shallots for the family. I dug more and more of the garden and began to sell the surplus vegetables at a time when there were posters up everywhere telling everyone to 'dig for victory'. On the field next to the ironmongers there was a small shed which belonged to the South Benfleet Allotment Association. I would go to the allotment shed on a Saturday morning and buy seeds. The seeds were in large bags and the seed was weighed and put in tiny brown bags. As I was the youngest member of the Allotment Association at twelve and a half years, the older gentlemen who used to serve me always gave me extra seeds. Onion seeds, which were black, used to be the dearest, and radishes, which were large round seeds, were the cheapest. You could get free books from the Ministry of Agriculture on how to get more vegetables from the ground. I used to grow huge Kos lettuces and a crisp one called Webbs Wonder. My father had built a greenhouse using glass crates and second-hand glass and I grew tomatoes called Ailsa Craig. They were fed with chicken manure and we produced a lot of them.

About 250 yards from our house was a general shop owned by a Miss Lacey, and I asked her if she would sell the surplus vegetables and tomatoes for me. She agreed, so each day I would set out the goods displayed on four wooden planks. The vegetables, which were freshly picked, sold like hot cakes and Miss Lacey took 25% commission for selling them. After a few months I was earning the sum of 25 shillings a week, a fortune for a boy of twelve and a half. I used to buy sixpenny savings stamps with the money I did not spend. You saved up 15/- to buy a savings certificate which would be worth 21/- in seven years' time which seemed like a lifetime to a boy of my age. I also had pocket money of 5/-.

I was fascinated with the idea of growing flowers for sale and I loved dahlias. I used to send for my plants from a firm called Stewart Ogg, and it was very exciting when they arrived. Each one had a hole in the garden dug in the winter and filled with manure. Stakes were put in and I used to de-bud the dahlias to perfect the blooms, which I sold. I joined the Royal Horticultural Society and one year I paid 25/- for a dahlia called Woodlands Wonder, a giant decorative dark red. My mother would have had a pink fit if she had known what I had paid for this dahlia.

In those days we wrote letters and paid with postal orders from the post office. I went to London with a specimen of Woodlands Wonder, carefully put in a cardboard box, and showed it at the Royal Horticultural Hall, where I got the second prize of 15/- and a certificate.

My parents were working every day and I was left on my own looking after my brother. I suppose I became a loner. I can never remember my mother or father giving me a hug or a kiss, although they bought me lots of things.

My own peace was shattered when the war finished in 1945 and the school was coming back home. After not going to school for 15 months I went back to Westcliff High School to continue my studies. I caught the South Benfleet Bus Company double decker at the Tarpots corner and the fare was sixpence return. We stopped at Hadleigh, where the bus garage was, and picked up a boy called Bridges who was the son of the owner of the bus company. I felt lost at school and I was landed with the hated English master Mr Midgely, who delighted in provoking me at every opportunity. One day he said to me 'Bishop, you will always be a failure and will not get on in the world.' I was so far behind that I left school at 14. I really wanted to go to the agricultural college at Writtle in Essex, but I failed the entrance exam.

CHAPTER 3

# Meeting Sheila

I decided to go into the family glass and glazing business. In no time at all I was able to cut glass and make leaded windows, and I decided to become an apprentice because I wanted to be the best.

The man next door, Mr King, had lost his wife in the war and lived with his only daughter. In 1946 he decided to sell his house, and it was bought for £1050 by a family called Daniels. Mrs Daniels looked quite a forceful woman. Her husband was not very tall, was thin and very quiet. They had a son, Bob, who had served in the Air Force and wanted to be a chicken farmer.

They also had a daughter who looked about 15. She wore brown slacks and a stripey yellow jumper which showed her figure. When she walked down the garden path I was drawn to looking at her. I had had no contact with girls before and had never thought about them. One day I was cutting the grass at the front of the house and I saw her looking at me over the fence. I had the collywobbles, but I plucked up courage and went over to the privet hedge and asked her if she liked living in Great Tarpots. She looked at me and spoke in a very nice voice, saying she had not wanted to move from her home, Garston in Watford, where she had been going to a very nice college. They had only moved house because her brother, Bob, wanted to be a chicken farmer. We talked for about 10 minutes. She told me her name was Sheila and I told her my name. She then said she had to help her mother get the tea.

Over the next few days, although I had not thought of girls before, I used to watch Sheila go down the garden. She distracted me, and after about three weeks I plucked up the courage to cut the grass in the front of the house again, hoping she would come out. I looked up, and there she was looking at me. I went over to the hedge and spoke to her again. She chatted and I asked her if she would like to go for a walk on Sunday. She said she would like to go very much. My mother said she had seen talking to the girl next door, and said 'you're a bit young to talk to girls.' I told her I had asked Sheila to go for a walk with me on Sunday and mother looked annoyed.

We went for our walk, which passed the house where I used to live, and chatted about silly things. I looked at her when she was not looking my way and thought she was a nice-looking girl. I had never been out with a girl before and felt I should like to see her again.

We said goodnight and suddenly I found myself asking if she would like to go to the cinema at Southend next Saturday. She looked at me, smiled and said yes. On the Wednesday I plucked up the courage to tell my mother. She said 'I don't like this really, you have never been out with a girl before.' She tutted and said 'you must be indoors by 10pm.' I went to work, but Sheila kept interrupting my thoughts.

Soon Saturday came and I put on the suit I had bought for one pound ten shillings from the shop on the parade. It wasn't new but it looked it. I also wore leather shoes, a tie and a handkerchief in my top pocket. I called for Sheila, and her mother and brother came to the door to sort of look me over. We caught the bus to Southend, she sat quite close to me, and I felt rather happy. I cannot remember the film we saw but the tickets cost 2/9p each and we had ice creams in the interval which cost threepence.

When we came out of the cinema, I said I would like fish and chips. She agreed and I bought two portions of fish and chips, one shilling and three pence each. We walked down to the gardens along the seafront, which were floodlit, and sat on a seat and ate our fish and chips. She smiled and said she enjoyed herself. I felt her eyes looking at me and I said we must go now or we would miss the bus. We got home just in time, and at the gate I said goodnight to her and she kissed my cheek and said goodnight. I had never kissed a girl or been kissed by one before and it felt good.

During the next few weeks, we went to the cinema on Saturdays and saw a lot of each other. In the evening she would walk down their garden and whistle. I had to think of excuses so that I could join her. My mother would say 'that girl is whistling again, but you are not going out!' It was very frustrating, but I managed to get out by saying I had to stoke the greenhouse boiler up.

We used to sit on a tree trunk down the garden, and one night she put her arms around me and kissed me on the mouth. She looked at me and said 'Well, put your arms around me!' I was spellbound, but she laughed and kissed me again. It was a lovely sensation, but I was worried because I knew nothing about the facts of life. I wasn't sure if kissing a girl could result in a baby. I told Sheila and she laughed her head off and said there was more to it than that.

We had been together for over a year now, and when we went out Sheila always put her arm in mine and I was quite proud of her. One Saturday we were home late and my mother and father were waiting at the gate and my mother laid down the law. Sheila just turned away and said goodnight.

On Sunday, after lunch, we used to cycle down the lanes to a place called 40 Acres where we sat on the grass and kissed. Sheila got my hand and put it on her bosom and said to feel it. I did and it felt wonderful. She laughed and lay back on the grass. I cuddled her and touched her breast again. She said to rub the piece in the middle, which I did, and I felt this hard piece in the centre and my willy began to grow. Sheila put her hand on it outside my trousers and rubbed it slowly up and down. I felt something happening and suddenly I was all wet down there. I knew nothing about sex, but Sheila taught me to excite her. Every Sunday we would go to the same spot if it was not raining and one Sunday Sheila said to put my hand under her jumper. She undid her bra so I could feel her. She was magic. I knew I loved Sheila. She had undone my trouser buttons and slid her hand over my willy.

I looked forward to this every week and she showed me other things to do to her which you would call heavy petting. One day, we went to the Kursaal at Southend. I took her on the roundabouts and we saw the wall of death. A motorbike would go up a wooden tower riding round and round. The rollercoaster was terrifying. We had some wonderful and exciting times.

Suddenly our happiness came to an abrupt end. Sheila said her brother could not make the farm pay, and he had lost most of his mother's money, so they were selling the house. They were buying a corner grocer's shop in Walthamstow in London. Sheila did not want to work in the shop, so she got a job in London working for a firm called Broadstreets British. The firm kept a record of all the directors and financial information about companies. If you were in business and were not sure if the company you were going to deal with had the money to proceed, this firm, for a fee, would give you all the information and the limit of credit they could have. I never knew such firms existed.

I was going to go to Hackney Technical College one day a week as part of my apprenticeship and I used to meet Sheila at Adelaide House right next to London Bridge when she got out of the office. I was always pleased to see her and gave her a hug and a kiss. We used to catch the number 38 bus to Walthamstow and I would have tea with Sheila and her family, but it was very frustrating as we were never alone. I persuaded my mother to let Sheila come to our house at weekends as we had a spare bedroom. We went for bike rides, walks and to the cinema. We were young, happy and in love. My mother gave up trying to separate us but kept a strict eye on us.

Sheila and I in 1950 Aged 19 years

We decided to get engaged and went to Samuels the jewellers in Southend High Street, where I bought a nice ring with a single diamond for £3.10s. I used to store my dahlia tubers in the other shed opposite the toilet and I hid the engagement ring in between the tubers. We had a spaniel called Rex and he got in the store and carried the box with the ring in it in his mouth and dropped it at my mothers' feet. When I got home from work, my mother said 'What is this?' I said it was an engagement ring and that Sheila and I wanted to get engaged. She stared and said 'in that case you had better announce it properly and we will have a small celebration.'

Sheila was coming down to stay the weekend and I told her the good news. All the relations and friends brought up presents and to this day, I still use the aluminium pots that were bought at Smiths the Ironmonger in the village and the roast pot which was given to us by Sheila's Auntie Jean.

Every other weekend I stayed with Sheila at Walthamstow and on Sunday morning we used to go to Petticoat Lane Market and buy things for our wedding. Arm in arm we would watch the stall holder, who would shout 'This lovely set of crockery, not £2 or £1, first 20 customers pay 15 shillings.' He would look at us and say 'I bet you two are courting'. Sheila would look embarrassed and said 'yes, we are engaged.' He said 'to wish you well on your way, you can have the crockery set and a teapot thrown in.' Of course I would feel in my coat pocket for the money and both of us smiling, took our box of goodies and ambled through the rest of the market wishing we could afford more of the lovely things on the stalls. Most of the stalls were lit by paraffin lamps.

We would go home for a roast dinner which Sheila's mother (a very good cook) would prepare, and then we would go for a walk. Sheila would hold my hand tightly and with her big brown eyes would smile at me and I would think how lucky I was to have such an attractive girl to be going out with and to eventually marry.

My mother's sister Mary lived at Sandgate, Folkestone in Kent and she wrote to us and asked us if we would like to have a week's holiday with Carl, who had been a German prisoner of war and who Mary had fallen in love with, to the disgust of the family. My mother thought about it and agreed to us going. Sheila's mother was also quite happy about it.

We both packed our suitcases and caught a train to Folkestone. Carl and Mary picked us up from the station, and although I had not met Carl before, and Sheila had not met either of them, we knew we were going to have a lovely time.

On the Saturday Carl and Mary got four tickets to go to the theatre in Folkestone. We were very excited as neither of us had been to a theatre. It was a variety show and we saw Arthur Askey, who was very funny; everyone in the audience heard all the popular songs accompanied by an electronic organ.

We had a meal in a small cafeteria overlooking the sea and we had a glass of white wine each. My mother would have done it in her knickers if she had known. It was a wonderful evening and after hugging Sheila and giving her a passionate kiss, we each went to our own bedroom, thinking how nice it would have been to have cuddled up close.

Carl worked as a builder and was very good looking and always smartly dressed. Mary worked in the local bakery, was kind and loved her husband very much (in complete contrast to my mother, who was smart, very attractive, worked all hours of the day, very ambitious and intended to go places in society and pushed my father). As Carl and Mary were out during the day, Sheila and I used to snuggle up on the bed, feeling and exploring each other. It was heaven, but no further than heavy petting. We wanted to save ourselves for our wedding night. It was a wonderful week, but all too soon it was time to say goodbye and catch the train home.

I used to meet Sheila on London Bridge. Sheila and her friend Pam used to trip down the slip from Adelaide House, laughing and talking. Sheila had bought a new coat. It was the latest new-look fashion in tweed herringbone. She looked lovely and had some admiring looks from men, much to my disgust. I was afraid her friend Pam would lead her astray and I would bubble with rage inside.

For several months I would see Sheila every weekend and every Tuesday evening, until one Saturday the phone rang and Sheila's mother said she was not coming down this weekend because she was unwell. I moped about all weekend, could not sleep properly and prayed for Tuesday evening. They both came out of their offices and Sheila said 'Hello Derek' and gave me a kiss. Some people going by gave us wolf whistles. Everything seemed all right and I went home happy. Sheila came down the next weekend and things were normal for the next few months.

We saw an advert in the paper for a day trip to Bologna in Italy for 25 shillings each. We had never been on a boat before except the one-hour trip around Southend on Sea. It was quite a rough crossing and I was as sick as a dog, but Sheila was fine. Once on dry land, I soon recovered and hand in hand we went around the shops and to the fairground. A Frenchman kept looking and winking at Sheila and it was with difficulty that she stopped me from giving him a bosh. It was a wonderful day. The trouble is I am insanely possessive of Sheila and I do not want anyone else looking at her. Sheila is mine alone.

I was just finishing my apprenticeship and sat for my City Guilds Certificate. I achieved a 90% pass, but then I received a letter from the War Ministry calling me up for national service. As a registered apprentice I had been exempt for two years. I told Sheila, and the next week she wrote me a letter saying she wanted to break our engagement as she did not want to go out with me any more. I was devastated and I pleaded with her, to no avail. I cried my eyes out. What was I going to do? I moped around for several months. My mother tried to get me to think about other girls, but I was not interested.

CHAPTER 4

# National Service

My call-up papers arrived and I had to report to Oudenarde Barracks in Aldershot. I arrived with five hundred others, and a Sergeant Major came out and shouted 'Get in line! What sort of a bunch have I got this time?' He glared at us and said 'I have got to get you lot to be soldiers in eight weeks, God help me!'

We went into a store room and were issued with our uniform and equipment boots. I had never worn boots. We marched off to some single-storey wooden sheds. Inside each were forty-eight iron beds with a metal locker beside each one and a boiler at the end of the billets, as they were called. A soldier with two stripes on his arm said 'I am Corporal Teeslate, and you are my platoon who I have to train as soldiers. You will now all file off to the barber for a haircut.'

I always had my hair reasonably short as I did not like my hair to tickle my ears. A lot of the others had curly hair, long hair and all sorts, as this was the time of the teddy boy cuts. The barber simply shaved the whole lot off and we all looked like convicts.

Next morning we were woken up at the unearthly hour of 6 am. The Corporal and Lance Corporal shouted at us to get up, get washed, get dressed in our uniforms and report outside at 7 am. When the

Corporal saw us we thought he was going to have a seizure. After ten minutes getting us in four ranks he then showed us how to stand upright and equally spaced apart. Now he said 'I am going to teach you how to march. This foot is your left and this is your right. When I say attention you put both feet together sharply. When I say by your left quick march, you start marching.'

We were all over the place. 'Halt!' the Corporal said. He came over to me and said 'What is your name?'

I said 'Bishop.'

'When you answer me you say 'Bishop, Corporal,' do you understand?' His face was very close to mine. 'Now hold up your left arm. When I tell you to march I say left quick march. Why do you put your right foot out?'

'I don't know,' I said.

'You will know by the time I have finished with you,' he grunted.

Over the next few weeks we were shown how to polish our boots to a mirror finish and level our cap badges with the buckles on our belt. We had to iron our trousers, which were made of coarse khaki material; the creases had to be sharp as a knife. We found out that you turned the trousers inside out and put wet soap up the crease, then turned them over and ironed them. A lot of my squaddies had never used an iron, and we had some fun with them.

Then one morning we had a Sergeant Major Underwood come to take us for drill. He soon had his teeth into me and would yell at me 'Bishop, your left! Your left!' He decided I was being awkward and I had to go back at 7 o'clock on the parade ground for extra tuition for four days. He said, gloating, 'By the time I have finished with you, one of us will be broken.'

One of the most revolting punishments I had to do was to scrape the urinals with a razor blade with the Corporal of the platoon standing over me sniggering and saying 'Bishop, get on your hands and knees, you've missed a bit.' He was right, because after four nights of this extra tuition and punishments I found I could march properly as instructed. He looked at me and gloated. 'I knew I could turn you into a marching soldier after eight weeks of training,' he said. The whole camp had a passing out parade in front of the Colonel of the regiment.

We passed with flying colours and were given a 24-hour leave pass with a train voucher. On arriving home I was given the once over by the family, 'So you think you are a soldier now,' said my dad. I changed into civilian clothes and went roller skating at Southend, but I ached to see and be close to Sheila.

I was back to barracks by 11.30 pm Sunday. On Monday morning we were assembled and marched to Headquarters to be interviewed to see who might be officer material. I got to the short list, but I did not have the right accent. I was to be trained as a clerk! We were taught how to word and set out letters and then we had typing lessons. They used to put a cover over the keyboard so you could not look at the keys, and then we had to type 200 words in twenty minutes without a mistake. I was told if I did not get it right I would have extra tuition 7pm to 8.30pm every day until I did, and no home leave.

My heart was not in it, and it took three weeks before I mastered it. I had to do fatigues in the cookhouse as punishment, wearing dirty denims, and to this day I will not wear denim because it reminds me of potato peeling and greasy pans.

I passed my clerk's course and was then sent on an eight-week course to learn shorthand typing. After three weeks I decided that I was not going to master shorthand and I was put on the short list for posting to a unit. I had two 24-hour passes, and on the last one I came back driving a five-seater Austin van which my father had loaned to me. On the next leave, I gave five of my fellow soldiers a lift in the van. I was driving across Hackney Marshes in London when a police car flashed its lights and I came to a stop. We were all hauled out of the van and I was questioned about it, as the police thought we had stolen it. After much discussion and checking the ownership of the van they said I was overloaded and had been driving at 34 miles an hour in a 30 mph zone. We pleaded we were National Servicemen and I was let off with a caution. When returning to the depot, I then got put on fatigues by the Corporal, as the police had been in contact with them.

Fourteen days later we were told to assemble in the parade ground as we were being posted. I was dumbfounded; I was being posted to Dispersal Unit Camp Fayed in Egypt. Where the hell that was I did not know. The next day we had to report to the medical centre for the inoculations against typhoid and malaria. You were given 48 hours to recover as these inoculations knocked you out. I did not feel too bad, so I got out of camp and came home. The family were amazed that I was going to Egypt. I went to Southend, visited the Odeon Cinema and had fish and chips. I walked along the seafront with its mass of twinkling lights and thought of Sheila. I could not forget her, even after six months. I took some photos with me, said goodbye to Mum, Dad and Tony and got back to Aldershot Barracks before I was missed.

These are the boys in Egypt. I am front left.

Eighty of us climbed into Army trucks with our kit bags and all the necessary documents and we were driven to Stansted Airport in Essex. Most of us had never been in a plane before and there sitting on the tarmac runway was a Boeing 747. The flight took eight hours including fuel refill stops, and we landed at the RAF airport, Fayid, in Egypt. On arrival we were quickly checked over, fed and then awaited our fate.

Me in Egypt 1951

A young National Service officer, Captain J.C.M. Staddon, inspected us and picked out eight soldiers including me and we all climbed in a 15-hundredweight truck with our kitbags and were driven along a windswept sandy road for about 15 minutes before halting outside a large security gate. We found we were in an area looking at the water of the Suez Canal. Grinding to a halt, Captain Staddon said 'You are now the detachment known as 107 Port Det RASC. 22594013 PTE Bishop, you have arrived!

Our living quarters in Egypt

In front of us were six army pole tents in khaki with iron bedsteads inside. 'These are your new quarters,' said Captain Staddon. After we had settled in, we took a look around us. There was a dirty old Army caravan with a sign saying 'OFFICE' by the side of the door. We then discovered that there were other tents and other soldiers on the camp. There was a building clad with corrugated iron which was the NAAFI and cookhouse. I have vivid memories of this building, which I will tell you about later.

We walked along the wall beside the Suez Canal. The sun was shining and the water was a spectacular blue. In front of us were six steam cranes which looked about fifty years old. The camp was surrounded by a barbed wire fence and in each corner was a sentry box about twenty feet up in the air. At the entrance was a small building that was manned by two soldiers to check identity, and it was used at night by the guards. Over in the corner, a building consisting of corrugated iron with no roof was the ablutions block. The toilets consisted of thick planks of wood with ten circular holes cut out to sit on. No privacy here! The shower facilities consisted of four 8-foot showers on a metal pole with a handle. No hot water here either.

Egypt 1951

The next morning we lined up in front of the Captain to hear our fate. To our amazement, Pte Newcomb was to be a clerk in the office and the rest of us were to unload the NAAFI supplies from the ships which docked in the canal. Each of us was given a lesson in how to count and check all the items being unloaded. We were each given one of these cranes and saw a barge dock by the side of the canal. I wondered how we were going to unload these ships with just seven of us.

What a surprise was in store for us at six o'clock the next morning. Attired in shorts, top and boots we were met with a squad of about sixty Africans; Tall ones, short ones, fat ones, all black as the ace of spades. I had never seen an African before except on TV.

'This is your workforce,' the official announced, 'fifteen each.' Each party consisted of a crane driver plus a corporal in charge and the rest were the labouring force. They certainly looked a strange bunch.

Fianera Wharf was just a concrete strip on the side of the Suez Canal with five of these weird-looking steam cranes. The large boats carrying the supplies for the troops would anchor in the Suez Canal and the barge would ferry the goods to the wharf, where there were lengths of rollers erected on wooden supports to transport the goods to lorries. It was our job to see to the unloading of the goods and check they were all there. The Africans, who we called 'wogs' at that time, could pinch anything and you would not know it had gone. I had never seen a black face before and I had a gang of fifteen who could only speak in broken English.

We started work at seven o'clock each morning. Sometimes we unloaded the NAAFI goods of beer, cigarettes, sweets etc. The Africans used to roll the crates along the rollers, and with everyone jabbering, crates of beer would be derailed and the Africans used to put the bottles in their mouth and bite the metal top off and guzzle and guzzle; gone in seconds. If a shortage was discovered we were put on a charge and lost some of our pay, so we had to juggle the loading dockets to balance. One time the crane driver dropped a case of cigarettes, and within seconds they had all disappeared. We unloaded diesel in two-gallon cans and flour in two-hundredweight sacks. We loaded five wagons with flour and all the wagons were sealed and boarded and the wagons put on the railway sidings. The next morning twenty tons of flour had disappeared without a trace.

The crane driver had to come in at six o'clock to get the steam temperature up to a certain level, otherwise the crane would not work. One day, the driver leaned out of the cab and said 'Johnny, the temperature is going up.' I said to him, 'Get on with the loading.' Five minutes later he said the temperature was still rising. I said 'Get on with the bleeding unloading.' The next minute he jumped out of the crane and I looked up to see the crane explode and fall into the canal. All work stopped and the Africans, seeing the opportunity, helped themselves to anything they could get their hands on. There was an enquiry, but I escaped with a warning, as I knew nothing about steam pressure on cranes.

I often looked at Sheila's photo and wondered what she was doing and whether she thought of me at all. I did truly love her and never got over her breaking off our engagement. But life carried on and I eventually became a Lance Corporal (one stripe) and every month I had to man the guard hut at night with two others plus a corporal. One night the Corporal said, 'Lance Corporal Bishop, proceed to the Sergeants mess cookhouse and light the boiler.'

Now there were three Sergeants who were former soldiers, called up under the Supplementary Reserves and sent out to Egypt. They were big tough men who didn't like National Service 'boys' as they called us. Anyway the cookhouse was on the end of their quarters and I went in to light the boiler. I turned the diesel tap on and lit the match and nothing happened. I tried again and still nothing. I went back to the Corporal and said 'I can't get the boiler to light.' 'For Christ's sake Bishop,' he roared, 'go and light the boiler!'

Back I went and turned the diesel tap again, but still it would not light. I thought 'I can't go back to the guardroom again' and then suddenly there was a whoosh and the cookhouse caught fire. I rushed out and shouted to the Corporal 'Corporal, the cookhouse is on fire!'

He had been sitting with his feet up but with no boots on. He roared, got stones and sand in his feet and rang the fire bell. The sergeants, half asleep, trooped out yelling murder. There was no water in the fire hose and no sand in the buckets. My fire burnt the building to the ground. I was put on a charge and marched before the Colonel of the regiment. I pleaded that I had never seen a diesel cooker before and was not aware they had to be primed before lighting. The Colonel eyed me suspiciously and demoted me to a private with the loss of a month's pay.

Soon after we received a shock announcement. Our little port detachment was going to be disbanded and I was being despatched to 148 Field Bakery Fayid. What a shock! I was put in a small office with two other clerks with Captain Barker in the other office. Captain Barker was a Yorkshire man and I knew we were not on the same wavelength.

It was my job to type all the replies to the numerous mailings he received. He was always picking some complaint about the layout or a chapter for signatures. A red line through a word and I had to retype. One day I had to type a five-page document, and when he found one mistake he said 'retype the lot again,' which I had to do in the evenings. I had had enough of this, so I typed it out again with about twenty mistakes. I stood there expressionless while he shouted at me 'Useless typical National Serviceman Bishop!' He demoted me to post orderly, which was the lowest job in the office, but I found that the job had its perks as I was in charge of all the mail arriving from other army depots and the mail from overseas. I was able to have extras in exchange for early delivery of the mail.

Every morning at 10 o'clock Captain Barker had a mug of tea and a plate of sandwiches. The other chap who worked with me in the office was a Scotsman, and we used to have a sandwich each and two sips of his tea before I took it in to the Captain. We filled up the mug with hot water. This went on for several weeks and we used to roar with laughter over this, but one day we got greedy and took three sandwiches, then rearranged the plate. Captain Barker decided to ring the Sergeant's mess where the tea and sandwiches came from to query why there were fewer sandwiches than usual. Of course we denied all knowledge. This was a close shave and we nearly came a cropper. Our new refreshments ceased!

After about six months I applied for 28 days leave to go to England. After a lot of questions about how I was going to pay for the flight, I said that my parents were going to pay and got a leave pass for 28 days. The flight was booked. I was quite excited to be going home on leave, but three days before going, Captain Barker called me into the office. With a smirk on his face, he said he was cancelling my pass for twenty-eight days' leave and only allowing seven days 'so in the circumstances it would not be worth it for you to go.'

I looked at him and had to keep my cool. I said 'even if it is for seven days I still want to go. I would like to see my brother who is ill with a kidney condition.' He gave me the leave pass for seven days with a warning if I was not back after that I would be put on a charge.

The flight from Fayid Airport on a British Airways Boeing 707 was very smooth and I arrived at Gatwick airport and travelled home on the train to Great Tarpots to see my family. After the second day I cancelled the return flight for 28 days. On the third day I tried to book a flight to return to Egypt within seven days. There were no flights available, so I rebooked the 28 days but went to the War Office in London and explained the position. They sent a wire to Captain Barker requesting extension of leave. The reply from Captain Barker was 'request refused, back in seven days.' The war office tried to get me on a troop ship. I enjoyed 28 days of leave; I even worked in the family business for 14 days and got paid. On the flight back, the plane diverted to Cyprus and I had to get off and find my own way back to Egypt. I booked in at the Troops holiday park in Famagusta and was just in time to queue for pay; I drew 28 day's pay. After seven days they were able to put me on a Corvette boat sailing to Port Said. I rang the depot to see if they could arrange transport and the answer was not printable – make your own way back! It took me three days to get back and when I entered the compound I was marched away and locked up in one of the guard tents.

The next day I was marched before Captain Barker, who said the charge was so serious I was required to appear before the Colonel of the regiment. The camp then ran a book on me, betting that I would get at least 12 months' detention. I said to myself, 'keep calm,' although I had collywobbles in my stomach.

The army had arranged a court for me. Left, right, left, right, I was marched in between two military policemen in front of the Colonel of the regiment. Some one and a half hours later, after I had given my side of the story, I awaited my sentence. The Colonel, who wore glasses, took them off, and then said 'Private Bishop, this is a very serious matter but after careful consideration I have a lot of sympathy for you. I am going to stop you 28 days' pay and confine you to barracks for 56 days. Case dismissed.' Captain Barker looked at me with evil in his eyes. When I returned to the depot, they looked at me in amazement. Most of them had lost their bets on me. There were two happy soldiers who had made a killing.

I went back to the office in fear of Barker, but then a stroke of luck occurred. Captain Barker was being recalled to England in 28 days. All I had to do was to be good during that time, which I was. After he went, we were left to await his replacement. The next day Captain Worthington arrived. I liked him and he took to me. Things started to change, and within six weeks I was promoted to Lance Corporal and put back in charge of the correspondence.

Captain Worthington had one major fault – he drank like a fish, and I found it was my job to look after him and get him out of difficulties. One day the phone rang to say the Colonel was on his way to do an inspection. What was I to do? I rushed over to the Captain's tent, where he was lying on the bed in a drunken stupor. I prodded him and said 'Get up! The Colonel is on his way.' He staggered up and I put a cloth soaked in cold water over his face and dressed him, put his cane under his arm and hoped to God he could make it. I watched him as he marched with the Colonel on the inspection of the Bakery depot, and as he passed me his eyes seemed to flicker, as if to say 'I have made it.'

About four weeks later, I was made chief clerk in the office and promoted to full corporal. Worthington was always under the influence of drink and he used to tell me about his unhappy home life. As I never drank any alcohol it was amazing how well we got on, although of course I always had to call him sir.

We had to render monthly returns of all stock held by the bakery, which used to take about four days to prepare, and I often wondered if they checked all this. On one report I made 500-gallon drums into 5000 and not a word was said, so we simplified the reports to less than a day's work by estimating a lot of the goods.

Time was marching on; I had only about three months left to serve and Captain Worthington only had six weeks to go. Our driver was a chap called John Davidson, who was being demobbed on the same day as me, and I decided it was about time we had a leave pass. It was part of my duties to make out leave passes. so I made one for myself and one for Davidson. I filled in the start date but left out the final finish date. I marched over to Captain Worthington, who was in his usual drunken state, and got him to sign them.

We decided we would go to Jerusalem, and got the train from Fayid to Port Said. Whilst we were wondering what to do next, we wandered into the small airfield, and were just looking around when a head popped out of this tiny plane and asked where we were making for. 'I can give you a lift to Oman,' he said. We both squeezed in behind the pilot, who gave us a pair of goggles each (health and safety would have had a field day). We looked at the barren nakedness of the land below us, and felt it was exciting. This was the first time we had been in such a small plane. It took about an hour to get to Oman. He dropped us off and continued his flight.

We then got a lift on a freight train and we sat with our legs dangling out of the sliding door. As the journey took about two days, we both slept in the train on the floor. I awoke during the night to find an Arab trying to molest me. I jumped up and hit him with my fists. John woke up and between us we hurled him out through the door. We finally arrived at the Goods Railway station at Bethlehem. The Arab taxi drivers surrounded us, asking 'Where do you want to go?' We said Jerusalem old city. We threaded our way through the narrow winding road with piles of rock and stone on the side. We then saw the old city wall of Jerusalem, just like the pictures in the Bible.

The taxi driver's cousin was an official licensed guide called Rajab Assab. We engaged him to find some accommodation and to look after us. He found a room in a small hotel opposite the Damascus gate, the main gate into old Jerusalem. The city of Jerusalem was in the rule of the Palestinians and there was a wired fence with a hundred yards of no man's land in between that and the other fence behind which the Jewish population were. Anyone setting foot in between got shot; on both sides, an uneasy tension existed.

The old city was exactly as it was described in the Bible. It had small caves cut into the rocks with steps cut between. All the caves were shops and workshops selling jewellery, clothes, food and gifts. On the third day I commissioned the shoe maker to make me a pair of shoes for my father, and John and I visited him every day to see how much progress he had made. We visited the tomb of Jesus in the Garden of Gethsemane, the cave he was walled up in, and the Dome. We went to Bethlehem to the Holy Church and kissed the golden star set in the floor. We went to Nazareth to see the underground cave where Jesus was born. We visited the Dead Sea, and I was quite scared as I could not swim, but the water was like brine and I found I was floating on top. We had a shower afterwards which was just a bit of rusty old pipe, with a piece of metal on top with holes punched in.

About four weeks later we were in the car when I saw a modern church being built. I asked Rajab to stop so I could see the builders. They were very excited to show us the cutting and laying of the stone walls. At one end I saw a workman fitting the glass to a window and asked Rajab to ask the man if I could help him. He nodded and I then proceeded to glaze 10 squares of glass to one of the windows. By this time about twenty labourers were watching me with amazement. They clapped and cheered, and then escorted us to their small glass shop in Jerusalem. I cut some glass for them and cut several complicated leaf shapes in green glass. After that word got around, and we were treated like royalty.

Every day we would sit in one of the gardens with orange, lemon and fig trees and eat a green watermelon with red flesh inside; delicious. After six weeks I thought we had better return to our unit, so I then filled in the return date on our leave pass. We shook hands with everyone and I collected the shoes for my father and bought my mother a black velvet shawl with gold embroidery.

We hitch hiked back to Fayid with just three weeks to go before being released from National Service. I had to be on best behaviour as the new CO was a 'paper man'; all forms in duplicate, letters by the dozen. Thank God we were going home!

On arrival in the UK we were sent to Bordon in Surrey to be finally demobbed. We were free at last – only to discover we were to keep our uniforms and kit bag because we had to serve two years in the Supplementary Reserve Army. We had to attend a camp twice a year for a fortnight's training. I then went home and back to work in the family glass business.

CHAPTER 5

# Early married life

Ithought about Sheila, wondering if she was married now and who she might be with; I did love her. Then after about eight weeks back at home, the phone rang and to my amazement, it was her. She asked how I was and said she would like to meet me. My heart was pounding so much I could hardly speak, and of course I agreed to meet her. She was working at the Law Society, so I arranged to meet her by London Bridge when she left work.

I caught the tube and waited nervously on the bridge. When she came walking towards me, dressed in her new-look herringbone tweed coat, her hair curled on the ends, to me she looked fabulous.

'Hello Derek, I'm so pleased to see you,' she said. We looked at each other, she came towards me and we embraced and kissed. Several people went by smiling and some clapped.

I said 'I thought you would be married by now.'

'I never forgot you Derek and I hope we can get back together.'

I was tingling all over and overjoyed with happiness. 'I've missed you dreadfully, you nearly broke my heart, but I think we belong together,' I said.

Sheila took me home to the house in Chingford in Essex that

they had moved to. Her mother and father welcomed me as though I had never been away. After making arrangements to see her again, I caught the tube to go home.

When I got home about 11.15 pm, my mother was waiting and said 'Where have you been?' I said I had been to see Sheila and we were going to get back together. Her response was 'After all the grief that girl has caused you, I can't believe it.' I simply said 'I never forgot Sheila, and as you know I have never been out with another girl and I love her.' She turned her back, muttering and went to bed.

I could not go to sleep. I was 21 and in love, and now I knew that all was not lost.

I met Sheila the following Saturday and we went to the cinema, holding hands in the dark and I could feel the warmth of her skin sitting next to me. She squeezed my hand hard and we kissed in the cinema. The couple behind us coughed and muttered 'Do you mind? we are trying to see the film.' We apologised and held hands tightly.

When we came out of the cinema, we had a fish and chip supper and went home arm in arm to her house, where I was going to stay the weekend. On Sunday, we went to Petticoat Market in London, and after deciding to get engaged again we bought several things to put away.

We were watching crockery being sold. 'Ladies and gentlemen, this crockery set would be £15 in Selfridges; I am not going to charge you anything like this. Who will start me at £5?' Silence. 'What's the matter with you lot? The first twenty people to put their hands up pay three pounds the lot!'

Now everybody was fighting to purchase the crockery sets and the lady on the stool took the money. Then he spotted us at the back 'Ha ha, what have we here? I bet you two are engaged.' We nodded and he smiled. 'Now ladies and gentlemen, this young couple, you can see are in love'. We blushed, the crowd roared. He said 'I've had a good day, and I'm going to help you on your way. I'm going to give you a dinner set and a cup and saucer set for the sum of two pounds.' My heart was thumping. I felt in my pocket for two £1 notes. I held up the notes and he gave us the two sets, wished us luck for the future and kissed Sheila. The crowd loved it; we moved away and left the market.

Sheila had kept all the engagement presents just in case. I used to meet her twice a week and she came down to our house every other week. My mother held her tongue and treated Sheila cordially.

I had £700 saved up and we decided to buy a plot of land and build our own place. We bought a corner plot of land with a 65-foot frontage in Hall Green Lane, Shenfield, Essex, which was some eight miles away from Romford. The plot cost £400 and we were helped by Mr Mason, the architect who had drawn the plans for my parents' new house. The purchase of the plot was completed on 30 March 1954. I drew a plan of the bungalow Sheila and I had designed and Mr Mason put the design together and submitted it to Brentwood Urban Council on the 18th April. We received planning permission on the 5th May (today it takes the Council 6-8 weeks just to acknowledge that plans have been submitted). We had to obtain a building licence from the Ministry of Works, and this was granted on May 12th with the condition that the total cost of the bungalow with its detached garage did not exceed £1500.

The plot of ground was overgrown with bushes and brambles and where the main bedroom was going to be there was a large oak tree. Sheila and I used to go to the site every day, after work and weekends, to clear the site. The bonfires we used to have! A friend of mine set the pegs in for the foundations and the pair of us dug out the trenches by hand.

On the 28th April we got a price from L.E. Lancaster, a local contractor, to concrete the footings (which Sheila and I had dug out by hand), lay all the drainage and carry out all brickwork to roof height for the sum of £189. We mixed up the cement with a cement mixer we had borrowed and concreted the foundation. We usually went home exhausted.

I purchased the second-hand stock bricks for the foundations from a church they were demolishing in Walthamstow. I had a bricklayer to lay the bricks and did all the labouring to keep him going. I made all the leaded windows for the bungalow. In the front of the lounge we had a large hardwood window with a smaller leaded diamond window with a running rose pattern incorporated. We had two semi-circular windows, one each side of the fireplace with leaded windows, one of the local church and a windmill in the other.

Sheila and I decided to get married on June 6th 1953. We were building a detached house next to the glassworks for my mother and father, so we would have to get married from the flat above the glassworks where they were living whilst the house was being built.

We got married at St John's Church, Gidea Park in Romford. What a day! Sheila's mother and brother were bringing her down, but the car they were travelling in had a tyre blow out and they were late. Everyone panicked. I was with the best man, Tony, and they forgot to send a car to pick us up. The best man drove us to the church and we arrived just after Sheila. We walked down the aisle of the church; she turned and smiled, looking radiant in her wedding dress. It was made by a friend of her mother and was satin brocade with embroidery stitched in with a train about nine feet long. She looked just like a film star. I was so happy to be marrying her at last.

This was a car my father bought after the war. A Hillman Coupe

After photographs were taken, we drove to the reception at 10 Main Road, Romford. The reception was for forty guests and the bill was £28 15s.

My father liked his cars and had just bought a new Zephyr 6 which he allowed us to borrow for our honeymoon. We were going to a farm in Combe Martin in Devon. We were so happy, but as we were going through Hampshire at about 11.45pm, the car stopped – we had run out of petrol. It was pitch dark, not a car to be seen, so we were isolated on our wedding night. After about twenty minutes a car came along and stopped and someone enquired if they could help. I explained to him that we had just got married and my father had let us have his car, but we had run out of petrol.

'You're lucky, I have a gallon can of petrol in my car,' said the driver. He put the petrol in for us and would not take any money; a wedding present from a stranger. 'If you go on for another two miles you'll drive into Stockbridge' he said. 'Go into the High Street and knock up one of the hotels.' We thanked him and glided into Stockbridge; block and red brick buildings one side and half-timbered buildings the other and three street lights. We knocked at one hotel with no response. Looking over the other side, we saw a sign over a tea place, 'The Three Cups'. We wondered if we should knock or not. We were very nervous but we pulled the handle and heard a bell ring inside. After about three minutes the bolts were drawn and the door swept open and there stood an old man wearing a nightshirt and a woolly hat. 'Yes, what do you want?' he said. I told him we were looking for a bed for the night. 'Just married eh? Come with me,' he said. With our luggage we followed him up the stairs and he opened the door and in the room was a huge bed, about 4 feet from the floor. 'You can have this room for the night,' he said, looking at us closely but with a twinkle in his eye. 'Sleep well.' We undressed and got into bed, I took Sheila into my arms and she snuggled right up to me. We made love and fell asleep with our arms around each other.

We woke up the next morning in this huge carved mahogany bed and I looked at the clock. It was 11.15. I said to Sheila 'Wake up sleepy head, it's gone 11 o'clock.' Adjoining the bedroom was the bathroom with a block white tiled floor, a large cast iron bath and a hand basin. The walls must once have been cream, but with age were turning brown. The hot water gurgled through the brass pipes. We got dressed and sleepily went down stairs to the dining room. The old man was now in a dark suit and with his wife, they looked at us and his wife laughed and said 'you must be hungry, I'll go and cook you something to eat.'

The two of us sat down at a large circular table with a white cloth, large linen serviettes and silver cutlery. We had a bowl of porridge each followed by egg, bacon, tomato and fried bread with a pot of tea and toast. We were the only two guests. It was lovely. We paid the bill, £2.12.6d. They both shook our hands and wished us a very happy married life.

Leaving Stockbridge behind us, we then motored to the farm at Combe Martin that we had booked for our honeymoon. After stopping several times for directions we went down a road and saw the farm's name. To my horror the approach to the farm was down a very steep narrow track; we could see the farmhouse down the bottom of the slope. I said to Sheila that we could not take the car down there, but the next moment a battered old Land Rover came up the track and a tall, distinguished man got out, smiled and said, 'leave your car at the top here and I'll pick you up daily. Just pip your horn and I'll be there.'

The farmhouse had five bedrooms and we were given the best one, as we were the only people staying. The husband of the lady who ran the bed and breakfast place, we discovered, was a distinguished scientist who had had a major nervous breakdown and they had bought the farm for him to recuperate.

Sheila and I made love twice a day; in the morning when we woke up and then when we went to bed. Writing this in 2010, I can remember every detail and even at the age of 79 I can still feel a hardening in my trousers. We fed the pigs at the farm and Sheila loved the baby lambs. Every day we went somewhere different on the beach. We did not swim but we paddled in the sea and walked on the soft sand of the beach, where we would draw letters about two feet high with sticks: 'Derek loves Sheila'. Every day the sea would wash it away, and every day we would lovingly rewrite the sign.

The week went very quickly, and after saying goodbye to our hosts, we made the long journey back to Romford, mercifully without any damage or scratches to dad's car. Quite a comedown arriving home, reality stepped in. We both went back to work and continued to build our bungalow.

Marley Tile Company tiled the bungalow with small tiles and a bonnet hipped roof for £129.15.6d. The carpenter did all the carpentry, including a solid constructed roof for £28.10. Those were the days! The house I live in now was built in 1991 and cost £196,000 to build. The cost of slate roofing was £10,750.

By the 17th June we had got a mortgage from the Council for £1250. By the end of July we were running out of money and I wrote to the Council asking for a further £250, otherwise we could not complete the building of the bungalow. The complete cost of the bungalow with a 20ft detached garage and including the quarter circle drive was £1800. On the 13th August the Council granted us the £250, giving a total mortgage of £1500 at 4.25 percent interest with repayments of £7.15 a month. We carried on with the completion of the bungalow and we were granted a certificate on the 20th April, handwritten by the surveyors' department, stating that in their opinion the dwelling was fit for human habitation. I still have the original plan and the costings of the bungalow.

Sheila and I had completed the self-build bungalow in 12 months including planning permission. Today, in 2011, we might have just received planning permission with a list of conditions about a page long.

This was the first building we had attempted, and the local council and building inspector advised and helped us during the construction. Today no help is available as the planning officers are frightened of making mistakes and the council of being sued. It was unheard of in 1954 for a council to be sued; that's progress. The rateable value set by the council on the 12th November 1964 was £27.

Sheila had stopped work now and was home in the bungalow. As I was only paid £7 per week it was a struggle to live, and we used to go to Romford Market on Saturday to get cheap veg and meat at the end of the day. I gave Sheila £5 and she struggled to make ends meet. We listed all our outgoings and I took it to my mother (who did the wages) and told her we could not manage. She looked at it for some time and said 'I'll increase your wage to £10 a week.' A sigh of relief, we could manage now.

Looking back now I was a bit bossy with Sheila, expecting her to feed me and look after all my needs. We had been married about nine months and I came home one day to find she had gone. She had taken all her things, all the furniture and left me only the bedroom suite and bed. I had to get my own meal and to go to bed on my own. I woke up in the night and felt for her and she was not there.

Next day I went to work but I did not say anything. This went on for five days, and then the phone rung and it was Sheila. 'Can I come home?' I said yes, but I wanted all the furniture put back where it was and a meal on the table when I got home. The removal men who had moved us in said to Sheila 'In, out, in, goes the furniture!' and scratched their heads and said 'we do hope this is the last time.'

I came back the following day and everything was back in place. Sheila had made steak and kidney pie, mashed potato and carrots. I came in the door, put my arms around her, kissed her with passion and said 'Welcome home.' We carried on as if nothing had happened and I did treat Sheila with a lot more thought and consideration.

I was energetic and I wanted the company to expand, but my parents were happy just to jog along, which resulted in a number of arguments between us. I would tender and undercut our rivals on contracts. My father, who was nearly bald, had a fringe of hair which nearly stood up when he saw the prices I had quoted. I also used to order twenty cases of glass from Belgium in order to get the best price, when he had been ordering just three at a time.

The firm expanded and we self-built a new factory at the back of our works with a large cutting bench in the middle. It had wooden racks all around to store all the different types of glass we stocked. No health and safety in those days. Glass was stocked everywhere, even cases were stored on the forecourt close to the footpath. We never had anything vandalised in those days. Our company was a pain in the neck to our competitors, as we used to undercut them on price and steal contracts from under their noses.

Sheila and I used to go to the cinema every Saturday, the Odeon in Brentwood High Street, and have a fish and chip supper afterwards. One day in June 1958 I came home and she said, 'Derek we are going to have a baby, I'm pregnant.' I looked at her in amazement, held her in my arms and hugged and kissed her. As it didn't show on Sheila, we did not tell our parents for another eight weeks. None of our neighbours knew.

On 30th December at about 11 o'clock we were watching a programme about Clive of India on the television which my parents had given us. Sheila said that she had got a pain in her stomach and it was happening every 30 minutes. I went and phoned the midwife who firmly stated that there was no need to worry. 'The baby will not arrive until tomorrow,' she said. I went back to look after Sheila. By midnight the pains were every 15 minutes. I rang the midwife again and told her that I would have her guts for garters if anything happened to Sheila. Within 10 minutes she arrived; Sheila's pains were now every eight minutes. The midwife examined her and said it was too late to go to the hospital. She said, 'You'll have to help me as the baby is ready to come.'

We stripped the bed sheets and put down a lot of newspapers with a waterproof sheet over the top. Sheila got in the bed and the midwife told her to lift her legs up and push. The midwife gave her some air from a pump she had brought, and as I stood there watching a small head appeared between Sheila's legs. 'Push, push!' the midwife kept saying to Sheila. What Sheila said to her is unprintable in a book like this. The baby suddenly came straight out, still attached by the cord. The midwife cut the cord, the baby yelped and was handed to me all covered in slime. The midwife attended to Sheila. She took the baby and I dashed to the bathroom to get a bowl of warm water and a flannel to wash her. The midwife gave the baby to Sheila and the baby suckled on Sheila's breast.

The midwife left at about four in the morning and we both fell asleep with exhaustion. We woke up about 10 o'clock and there was a loud bang on the door. Bossy boots the midwife was standing there. She had come to wash the baby and tidy up Sheila. I made three cups of tea, one for Sheila, one for myself and one for the midwife. We sat down and I said to her that if she had not come I would have made her life hell. She glowered at me. I looked at her and said 'we have a lovely baby girl'. Then I shook her hand and we were friends.

My mother and father had brought a top of the range Silver Cross pram. We decided to call the baby Karen Sheila. She was very good and only cried when she was hungry. The neighbours were astonished that we had had a baby and we had several presents from them. Opposite us an elderly lady who lived on her own gave us a small glass vase with anemones in it. I am writing this at the kitchen table and I can look at the vase, which will have anemones in it in December again after 50 years.

CHAPTER 6

# Fernside

Time went by and baby Karen was talking and the business was prospering, but I always dreamed of building houses. At the bottom of our road a butcher lived in a nice house and he got permission to build nine houses in his garden. I was very excited to buy this land and with the support of Sheila, he agreed to sell me the land for £8,500. My parents would not lend me any money as they did not want me to build houses; they wanted me to stay in the family glass business.

We put our bungalow up for sale, and with a bank loan, we were able to proceed with the purchase of the land. We exchanged contracts on our bungalow within six weeks and 14 days after that the butcher sold the land to someone else for £1000 more. We were devastated, and Sheila screamed at me 'what are we going to do now?'

I approached my parents, who said we could have the flat above the glassworks rent free. Sheila was not happy, but I said it was only temporary until we could sort something out. A detached house came on the market on the main road which had been requisitioned by the armed forces and was now empty. I bought it for £2200 and did it up. I built a garage, new bay windows, new bathroom and a glass conservatory the width of the house. Sheila refused to help me with this house and when we completed it she refused to move in. She was stubborn – we had a new bungalow and I wanted another bungalow or a new house. Sheila would not budge, so I had to sell the house for £7800. I felt deflated and continued working in the glass business.

I used to make a lot of leaded windows of differing designs, such as roses, tulips, galleons and windmills. I used to go over to my mother for a cup of tea when Sheila was out shopping. One Friday the local paper was on the table and I glanced at the property page. I saw an auction announcement for a Victorian mansion called Fernside, built in 1890. It sat in four acres of land and was in need of lots of renovation. It was just outside Romford at a place called Fernside,

Fernside. Havering-atte-Bower, Romford

Havering-atte-Bower. I thought to myself that I would have a look at it without telling Sheila.

On the Saturday morning, I drove to Havering-atte-Bower to look at the house. I drove up to the village, which still had a set of stocks on the village green outside the church. I turned left past a cricket ground and saw a sign which said 'Bedfords Park'. Next to the entrance to the park I saw two huge granite pillars and a pair of wooden gates with rough iron spikes on the top. The gates were all covered with moss and green slime, although they had been white many years ago. I opened one of the gates, which creaked and groaned, and stepped into another world.

The wilderness in the front was covered with brambles and broken-down trees. Peeping above this I saw the gable of a house with a leaning chimney breast on top which was completely covered in ivy. Most of the slates on the roof had gone and all the windows were broken. I forced a way around the back and stepped into the house through a bay window, and in front of me was a big hole in the floor. Someone had tried to set fire to the house. I crept around the room and opened a door which revealed a beautiful staircase with a balustrade handrail with a carved snake piece on the end. The ceilings were all intact with plaster carved coving and plaster sets around the lights (there were no signs of any light fittings at all).

I opened another door and to my astonishment I saw black cobwebs cascading from the ceiling and touching the floor. I hurriedly shut the door and found another door into a room in which there was a toilet pan with a wooden top with a hole in it. The brown stains and the smell were revolting. I then ventured up the stairs and at the top was a large cast iron bath, which would have been white many years ago. It had an oval washbasin and bare floorboards. There was a small semi-circular window with plain glass, and looking through I saw a large square area which was covered with large tufts of grass about 3 feet high and a row of trees running around the boundary. The landing was quite spacious with four spacious bedrooms. I felt quite excited. What would it be like to own a house like this; a miniature lord of the manor?

I came out of the house and looked around the grounds. I have always been fascinated by monkey puzzle trees, there was one about 40 feet high. Close by there were two more huge trees about 60 feet high with a girth of about 8 feet. The bark was not of a normal tree but was in half rounds going right up the tree. I put my arms around one of the trees and found the bark was soft and spongy. I thought, my God these trees are so rotten and will fall down and smack into the house. Later I found that they were Wellingtonias from Australia and could grow to 130ft high and live for 150 years. The bark was one of their special qualities.

I then found a block of outbuildings. On opening one of the large double doors, I found myself in a large area with a block floor with recessed sections about two feet wide. This was where the coach would have been garaged and the wheels would have fitted into the recesses. Next door were the stables for the horses and the other section was where the coachmen lived. The remainder of the grounds was inaccessible, but the views from the grounds were breathtaking. You looked right over Romford.

My next problem was, how the hell I would convince Sheila it might be worth bidding for? I returned home, my stomach churning and wondering how to broach the subject. Sheila looked at me and said 'you have been up to something. Let's have it!' I said 'Well, I have just looked at a house, it needs a bit of doing up but it might be worth a look'. It was now five o'clock on Saturday and she said 'I'll come with you and look at it tomorrow. We can leave Karen with your mum and dad.'

We went to bed about 11 o'clock and I snuggled up to Sheila and we made love. I felt very contented and went to sleep dreaming about the house.

On the Sunday we left Karen with Mum and Dad and drove up to Havering-atte-Bower and I pulled up to the gates to Fernside. Sheila looked at me, sighed and said 'What have you brought me to?' I put my arm in hers and said she should prepare herself for a surprise. 'Think what this house could be,' I said.

Sheila walked slowly towards the house and went in, taking it all in and saying nothing. I thought, that's done it, I've had it now! We went round the grounds as best we could and I showed her the magnificent view. We got back in the car and I waited with bated breath.

Sheila looked at me and said, 'Knowing what you could do with this house, and against my better judgement, I agree to you going to the auction.' She smiled and kissed me. We went home to our temporary flat and I broke the news to my parents. I was going to try to buy the property. My mother poo-pooed the idea, but the auction was the next Friday at 11 o'clock at the White Hart Hotel Romford.

During the week I gathered all our finances together; we had £7800. Would we get it? I felt we had to get this house. After a week of not sleeping well, Friday arrived. Sheila decided not to come along. I put my best suit on, tie and handkerchief in pocket, and entered the White Hart Hotel (which was built in the 1800s). I went under an arch, through a timbered door and a notice said 'Auction this way'. I went into this room and there were about twenty people there and I was the youngest one in the room, the next oldest being in their 50s.

The auctioneer announced the auction of Fernside. 'Do I have a bid of £5000?' Someone nodded. It went to £5500 and then to £7000. I was sweating and bid £7500. Everyone looked at me and there was a hushed silence. '£7500, any advance? Going once, going twice'. Someone said £8000. I bid £8250. Another bid of £8500 was made. Although it was more money than I had, I bid £8750. 'Going once, going twice'. Down went the hammer. 'Sold to the young man in the fifth row. Please come forward so we can take your particulars and pay the 10% deposit.' The rest of the audience clapped me and shook my hand, congratulating me on securing Fernside.

I left the White Hart elated, thinking I had got 28 days to complete and find another £900. Arriving home Sheila was waiting for me. 'Well did you get it?' I threw my arms around her and said that I had, but the bad bit was that I had to find another £900 in 28 days. My father, on hearing my predicament, gave me the £900, and Sheila and I became the owners of Fernside.

Sheila had some savings and we raked up £600 to start doing the place up. The first job was to clear the front of the house of brambles and overgrown trees. I chopped it all down with a sickle and saw and we had a huge bonfire. We discovered a circular drive to the house. The next job was to clear all the rubbish and sweep out the house to see what we had bought.

The only way I would be able to make this house hospitable on the money we had was to employ tradesmen who I knew in the building industry and pay them cash to work at weekends and evenings. Sometimes we had 15 men working, and Sheila made them tea and sandwiches. We had a chimney stack rebuilt and I incorporated two windows with half-circular tops which came from a church. I got them in the scrapyard for four pounds. I made the square leaded windows and we made that room the kitchen, and the room above our bedroom. I bought a hundred rolls of anaglypta wallpaper and all the walls in the house were done in the same paper and emulsioned in differing shades. The kitchen was made by a carpenter friend of mine and it looked superb. I will not bore you with the amount of work Sheila and I did, but it took about 12 months before we could move in.

Karen went to the local school and soon settled in. Sheila joined the Women's Institute (WI) and a chap called Bob Manton called and persuaded me to help him with the fete which was held on the village green. After about two years I had got the grounds under control. Sheila settled in, but found it was a bit quiet. She made friends in the village and visited them during the afternoons. Bob Manton and I found a small band of helpers and we called them 'The helping hands of Havering'. Over time Sheila and I became very involved with the activities in the village. I used to supply all the wood and paint needed and the volunteers made all the sideshows in the stable block. I used to use one of the firm's lorries to transport everything.

Bob Manton, our chairman, was manager of a Bata shoe shop in Grays in Essex. He was married to Vera, an Italian, who was highly strung and extremely volatile. Bob and I were putting the arrangements together for the annual village fete when we were faced with a problem. We had just been given a hundred goldfish, but where were we going to put them? Bob said we could take them to his home and put them in the bath temporarily. All was well until Vera, half naked, decided to take a shower and gave a shriek, shaking her fists at us! 'Good God,' I said, 'she's on the war path!' We bolted out of the house and she was shouting at us 'Get those fish out of this house by five o'clock or do not come home.'

I remembered an old water butt I had at home and we transported the fish to my place. It was a good job Vera could not see us, as we could not stop laughing.

Bob was always looking for different sideshows for the fete and he decided to build a contraption to be called 'The Mighty Quin'. I supplied the wood and this thing was about six feet high and ten feet wide. It was a collection of cut-out figures held together by ropes. You paid ten pence and put your foot on the pedal and all the figures would dance. Everybody started to sing 'Bobby's Mighty Quin, ooh-la-la!' All went well until one of the punters put his boot hard on it and the whole thing fell apart. Everyone there sang 'This is the end of Bobby's Mighty Quin, ooh-la-la.'

My wife was the treasurer and we made over £450 profit for the local hospital. Unfortunately, at our next fete, everything was in place, but we woke that morning to our worst nightmare, it was raining hard and continued until four o'clock. The sun came out and the fete got back on track. Fortunately we had insurance against rain and we got back £400 from the insurers. We did not tell them we had continued with the fete; happy days.

Bob was Chairman of the Havering Multiple Sclerosis (MS) Society and asked me to help him, so I was appointed Vice Chair. We saved up enough money to buy an ambulance from London County Council and we used to take the MS members out on an outing to Southend on Sea. I bought an ex-army marquee and held parties in our garden. We decided to put the marquee up on the village green, and as we did not like to look like idiots we had a trial run in the field at the back of the garden. We got the marquee up and my job was to hammer in the pegs. I said to Ken 'Hold that peg while I knock it in the ground.' I missed it and hit his hand. He ran around the field shouting and swearing, while the rest of us laughed till tears rolled down our faces. He was none too pleased.

Once a year the MS committee had to entertain the members, and Bob as usual dressed up, something that terrified me. We were to dress up as two boys in shorts and braces and sing 'Two Little Boys'. I cannot sing a tune and cannot remember the words of a complete song. Sheila, who had a lovely singing voice, drilled me for three weeks. I must have sung 'Two little boys had two little toys' about a thousand times. When the entertainment took place they announced the star turn, by Bob and Derek! God, I was in a panic. We both came out dressed up as two little boys and the music started. I had Sheila in the wings behind the curtain miming the song in case I forgot the words. The members clapped and laughed, especially when Sheila came out from behind the curtains.

A Canadian ex-army lorry my father converted into a glass lorry.

Sheila and I were coming up in the world now. I was appointed School Governor to the two smallest schools in the Romford Area, Dame Tipping School in the village and St John at Stapleford Abbotts.

All the time we lived in the village I never missed a single meeting or school sports day. The children used to make us cakes and a cup of tea, and it gave us a close relationship with the schools. We had three trustees and our chairlady was the Mayoress of Romford, Angie Smith, so we were able to obtain a lot of equipment and things for the schools.

Sheila and I went to Romford to see a Donkey Derby and came back with the bright idea of running one in the village. We called our small band of helpers together to discuss the project and as usual Bob dreamed up a lot of fantastic ideas. I arranged with the local farmer to have the use of a fifteen-acre field at the end of a narrow track. As this was the largest event we had held, we hired a marquee and a tea tent and booked donkeys from a firm in Lowestoft. We phoned around and were able, through Mr Smith the Mayor, to book a mobile toilet block from Thurrock Council.

Everything was going well and brochures were printed, but on Monday 2nd September 1968, the day of the Donkey Derby, things started to go wrong and I was getting hot under the collar. The toilets arrived, they were about twenty-five feet long, but we could not get them into the field as the gate was too small and there was a tree in the way. I made the quick decision to saw the tree down having no idea what the farmer would say.

The Mayor, who was going to open the event, was due at 2pm, but by 1pm there were no donkeys. The betting tote was in position and all the side shows were manned and the sun was shining, but where the hell were the donkeys! Sheila ran home to ring the donkey owners, and rushed back out of breath to say that they had caught the flu and another group were coming from eighty miles away and would arrive about 2.40pm. I swore under my breath that when I got hold of the donkey man I would break every bone in his body.

We were all dressed up when the Mayor's Rolls Royce arrived at precisely 1.55pm. The Mayoress stepped out and I welcomed her. I said 'Your Worship, we have a problem. The donkeys have caught the flu and the replacements will not arrive for about another 40 minutes.' She said 'Not to worry Derek.' Fortunately my mother, who was the Vice Chair of the Council, was a close friend, so the Mayor circulated round the sideshows.

Then two large lorries arrived with the donkeys and I went racing up the field to give the driver hell. The driver smiled and said 'Got the donkeys here for you. Show me where they are to go and I will set them up for racing. Leave it to us; we could do with a cup of tea.' I nearly choked but saw the funny side, relaxed and laughed.

The Mayoress started the first race off and at the end of the afternoon we had taken over £750. Everyone went home exhausted. A week later we received a letter from one of the spectators to say that he had caught the sump of his car over the tree stump and he was going to sue us. I went to see him, as we only had a limited insurance policy and said that if he sued us we would have to publish it in the local paper that no money could be paid to the local Children's Home because we were being sued. He stuttered but agreed to claim from his own insurance company. Instead of going at it like a bull in a china shop I was very diplomatic, and it took some doing, I can tell you.

Sheila, who was a member of the WI, suggested we might have a firework night in the donkey paddock (I'll tell you about the donkey later). I said it was a good idea, so I brought home two lorry loads of wooden glass cases from our glassworks. The glass we imported in from Belgium came in wooden cases about four foot wide and nine foot long. I put them together like a wigwam and we had some hot dogs, rolls, fried onions and cakes of all sorts, tea and coffee plus lemonade for the children.

About twenty ladies with their husbands and children turned up. The coloured lights round the garden looked superb. I lit the paper at the fire, and flames fifteen feet high towered up into the sky! I had two boxes of fireworks; sparklers in one and bangers and jumpers in the other. We were all around the fire when there was a huge bang behind us – the fireworks were exploding and the sky lit up. What a show! Some of the older members of the WI had never moved so fast in their lives. A spark from the fire must have landed in the banger box. It certainly livened up the party, and we still had the sparklers left. The WI must have enjoyed it, as it was mentioned in their newsletter.

Now to get back to the donkey. Karen had started riding lessons and wanted a pony but I thought she might get fed up, so I bought a donkey called Noaly for twenty pounds. I thought that if she looked after it for a year I would then consider buying a pony. Karen used to ride it around the village and all seemed to be going well. Noaly did not like me; perhaps she sensed that she was only there temporarily. I wired a section of the field off for a donkey paddock – it was supposed to be stockproof, but she used to torment me by getting out. One day the phone rang and a voice enquired if we had lost a donkey. Looking into the paddock I could see no donkey, so I said yes. The donkey was about a mile away. I rang my friend Bob and he came around in his car, and we found a big piece of rope and went to get Noaly. I thanked the lady – fortunately no damage had been done.

Then I came up with the brainwave of putting the rope into the halter around his neck and got into the back seat of the car with the window open, pulling Noaly behind the car. As you can imagine the neighbours came out to see the fun. All went well, and Bob was driving about ten miles an hour, but when Noaly decided to stop to wee, the rope stretched and my head was pulled through the window. 'Stop!' I yelled at Bob, who could not stop laughing.

We got going again and fortunately no cars overtook us. I thought it was just as well that no one could see me. When we got to our gates and turned in, half the village were there clapping and laughing. 'Here comes the donkey man,' they sang. It took me some time to get over that. The novelty had gone for Karen and muggins here had to clear out the stables and buy all the food and straw, so I sold Noaly for fifteen pounds.

The glass business was going very well. We had glazing contracts all over Essex, but even with our new factory at the rear of our shops, we were short of space. We used to buy in sheets of second-hand glass from a London firm who could not store them. I had two lorry loads delivered to Fernside and put into one of the stables. I would come home for lunch and say to Sheila 'You'll have to help me while I cut up two sheets of glass.' I would measure the glass and Sheila would hold the batten of wood while I cut the glass with my Red Devil wheel cutter. Then she would have to hold the glass while I put a batten of wood behind the cut and then I would put both hands on the glass and push hard. The glass would snap and Sheila would hold one end of the glass and help me put it on the lorry. Not many women would be able to do this. She did love me you know, and looking back I did not appreciate her enough.

We secured a large contract for the installation of some 12,000 square feet of glass to a factory in Saffron Waldon in Essex. We did not have enough men to do the job, so my father had to work as well. They built an office which overlooked the factory so that the manager could see everything that went on. We had to fit a plate glass window eight feet high and nine feet wide and it had to be hoisted twenty feet up a stairwell with two inches to spare each side. If the glass touched the side it would fracture. There were six of us and I needed eight men, so I asked two of the builders if they would give us a hand for two pounds each.

I put a blanket over each side and we got the glass in position to put in the frame. The sweat was pouring off me. When the glass was put in the frame it was a quarter of an inch too big, so I had to get up on a pair of steps and cut a quarter of an inch off. When the contract was completed we received an invitation from the directors to attend the opening ceremony, which was going to be opened by the Minister of Works, Paul Channon MP. The general foreman kept looking at us, trying to remember where he had seen us. We were both dressed in our best togs and did not blink an eyelid. Our small firm had got away with competing with the major glass firms. John Bishop and Son Glaziers Ltd – who the hell were they? We were on the map.

I used to do the estimating and if I wanted to get a contract I would gamble and cut the price to the bone. My father used to rant

Nice looking, but not that good 'aye'

and rave and I used to say to him to stick to the office, and if we lost money on a contract he could take it out of my wages. I used to work like hell to make sure we made a profit.

Sheila used to moan as I sometimes worked to eight o'clock. One day she said to me, 'How is it that the men have a holiday but you're always working?' I thought about it and said to my father that Sheila wanted a holiday. I asked, 'Shall we close down for one week?' Nothing could go wrong as we would be closed.' Unbeknown to us at that time, the decision we made would change our entire life.

I asked Sheila where we should go, and we decided to go to Cornwall.

## CHAPTER 7

# Moving to Cornwall

❖ — ❖

The three of us piled into our car, a Rover 2000 TC, and we headed for Cornwall. We arrived at Looe and saw a signpost pointing to Polperro. Although we had never heard of it, we followed the road down a steep winding hill, and parked in the car park at the bottom before walking down the main street, which got narrower and narrower. It was crowded, with people everywhere.

We went round a very sharp corner and came to Polperro Harbour. I said to Sheila and Karen, 'this looks nice. Shall we stay for bed and breakfast for one night?' All the cottages had 'full' or 'full no vacancies' signs up. We knocked on one house in the centre of the village and the person pointed us in the direction of the house opposite. I knocked on the door and a pleasant lady with glasses said we could stay the night. Her husband was a German prisoner of war, Heinz Valkelt, who had married a Cornish girl. They made us very welcome, and they had a daughter called Katherine who was the same age as Karen. We were able to put our car in the Claremont Hotel car park opposite.

The next day, liking Polperro so much, we decided that we should stay the week and travel around Cornwall from there. We went to the beach at Talland Bay with Heinz and Maureen and had a whale of a time (although it was too hot!) It was like entering into a different world. It was the first time I had relaxed in many years.

We were sad to say goodbye to the Valkelts and when I went back to running the glass business, I found I could not settle. The holiday in Cornwall had showed us a different way of life. The following year we went back to Polperro and stayed with Heinz and Maureen again. The weather was glorious and we travelled all over Cornwall, but we liked Polperro the best. We looked at all the artist's shops with their variety of paintings and souvenirs.

We walked up a steep slope to a small building and looked inside, where I saw a painting the Italian Dolomites. I said to Sheila. 'Look at that painting. Shall we ask the price?'

The shop owner came out from behind a screen. He had a short beard and wore an overall covered with various colours of paint. 'That painting is sold,' he said. He explained that that artist, whose name was De Marco, only did three or four paintings a year, all of the Dolomites. We said to him 'Do you think we could commission him to paint one of our Victorian house?' We showed him a photo of our house and said the size would be about three feet high by four feet wide to go above a Victorian marble fireplace. He phoned the artist and said he would take on the commission and it would take about 12 months and cost approx. £120. I paid a £50 deposit. We felt quite excited to be able to actually commission a painting.

Polperro is set in a valley with steep slopes both sides of the road. We saw a piece of overgrown land on the side of the hill and I said to Sheila 'How about that land for a holiday home?' She agreed with me and I asked Heinz who owned it. He said it belonged to Jimmy Beddoes, who also owned the car park. I asked Heinz if he could make enquiries as to whether the land had planning permission for building or whether Beddoes wanted to sell. It turns out that Beddoes would sell the land, which did have planning permission, and he wanted £1500.

Sheila and I decided to give the site a closer look. It was fantastic with a view of the sea, but very steep with about a 45 degree angle. We made an offer about three months later at £1400, but he refused, so we decided to pay the full asking price. We then started sketching various plans for a split-level house. We were only used to building on flat land, so I engaged a draughtsman to put the plans together. We came up with a building ninety feet long and thirty feet wide with an angled twenty-foot window in the lounge and a basement area eighty foot by twenty-five foot with a six-foot-wide balcony running along the rear of the property. We submitted the plans and after about five months we received planning permission in the post.

I could not settle now to running the business and we both thought about potentially moving to Cornwall. I spoke to my father and mother about it. They did not want us to go, but said that if we could sell the business that would help. With the help of the accountants, we negotiated with a public company called Winn Industries. They bought small profitable firms and had three companies in Essex; we would fit into the building supplies mould. My father and I had to go to Grosvenor Street in London, which was the head office. The Chairman was a man called John Howard, a real gentleman with a cravat. He made us very welcome. After much discussion they agreed to buy the shares in the company for £60,000, but I had to run the company for seven years – no me, no sale. I agreed, and my father was happy as he was getting on and enjoyed bowling four times a week, and I think he was looking forward to retiring. We had to go to London again and the contracts were duly signed. I altered the seven years to three years, and no one noticed. I was sweating, I can tell you.

I was allowed to run the business in the usual way but I had to do a monthly report and the area director came over from the Abbey Tile Company in Barking to check that I was running the business properly.

I was invited up to Grosvenor Street in London for the Christmas meeting of the various companies in the group. At about 11 o'clock that night the chairman asked me to take another director (who was the worse for wear) to the station. I called a taxi and he decided that we should go to a health club in Kensington. I protested, but he said I would enjoy it.

We arrived at this place and entered through a large carved door into a basement area, thick with clouds of steam and half-naked men walking around. I had never seen anything like it. He was well known there; he took off his clothes, put on a Turkish bath robe and went into this room filled with steam. He asked me to come in, but I was nervous and said no.

When it got to 12.30 I asked the attendant to find out when he was coming home. It seemed he was staying the night, so I arrived home at 2.30am, slid into bed and snuggled up to Sheila. What an experience, I realised I had been set up!

The next day I telephoned his wife to make sure he had got home. She laughed and thanked me for phoning and said this was a regular occurrence and she was well used to his jaunts.

I was reading *Daltons Weekly* one day and saw that under Land for Sale, 102 building plots were for sale at Pensilva in Cornwall for £28,000. I phoned Heinz in Polperro and asked him to have a look at the site and describe it to me on the phone. It sounded perfect. The problem was I had to raise £28,000. The accountant arranged a meeting with a Mr Raithburn at the NatWest bank. I entered the bank with butterflies in my stomach. I was led to Mr Raithburn's office, where a tall, distinguished man of about sixty shook my hand and asked how he could help me. I showed him the particulars of the land and explained I wanted to build properties for young people.

'If the bank lends you the money, how are you going to fund the building of these bungalows?' he asked.

'By selling my house and moving to Cornwall,' I replied. 'Well young Bishop, having seen your manner and enthusiasm today, I shall recommend the bank loans you £28,000 with security on the land,' he said. He shook hands with me and wished me every success in my new venture.

I walked out of his office and went home to tell Sheila, 'I have got the loan to buy the land. How do you feel about moving to Cornwall?' We completed the purchase of the building plots and I employed Heinz on a one-year contract as a site agent to build the first stage of 28 two-bedroom bungalows at a selling price of £2895 each. This was our first venture under the name Kean Estates, Karen Homes. We then decided to start construction of our new home in Landaviddy Lane, Polperro, which being a complicated site with the slope required deep foundations on shelfed grounds. Heinz would engage the workers and supervise the site. It was a long journey to Cornwall, but we went down every month. I ran the glass business in the week, travelled down Friday night and got back to Romford for 9 am on Tuesday morning.

We had built a show bungalow at Pensilva with a landscaped garden with a fountain. We sold the first bungalow to two retired sisters called Moncton. We had the Mayor of Liskeard for the opening ceremony and Karen handed over the keys to our first bungalow with a free gift box from the electricity company and a bouquet of flowers. We now had deposits on ten bungalows.

The Polperro bungalow was progressing by leaps and bounds, but suddenly out of the blue I had a telephone call from Henry Tucker, our architect, who said we were to come down to Cornwall to see the chief planning officer. who was complaining that we were building a three-storey building and he was going to post an enforcement order on the bungalow to knock down about a third of it. We arranged to meet him on a Friday afternoon at three o'clock to discuss the situation.

We travelled the 350 miles from Romford and were in Polperro by 2.45pm. No planning officer on site. At 3.20pm a car pulled up and a man got out and approached us. He said the bungalow was not being built to the approved plan, as we had erected a retaining wall in Cornish stone to form a base to build the bungalow on top. This, he said, created a three-storey building and he was going to put an enforcement order to demolish it. He would not listen to my explanations of how this could be overcome, so I said to Henry Tucker, 'I can't talk to this man. I will leave you to deal with the situation,' and we jumped into the car and drove off. My wife said 'You've done it now, and we haven't even got to Cornwall.'

On the way home I had a brainwave. We had just started work at Tremar Coombe, a small village outside of Liskeard. They were removing the top soil to store it, so I arranged for forty lorryloads of topsoil to be sent to Polperro and be tipped over the site, covering up the retaining wall, which got rid of the problem. The Council were unhappy, but they allowed us to finish the bungalow. However we did not know that the same planning officer would be supervising our building projects in Cornwall.

We had taken a trip up to the Ideal Home Exhibition and were looking at exhibits when we came to the Waring and Gillow stand and saw some fabulous carpets. A gentleman came up to us and asked if he could help us. We said we were building at Polperro in Cornwall but the build would not be ready for over a year. He said 'no problem sir, we can reserve this carpet for you for a hundred pound deposit and the balance on fitting.'

We showed him the plan; we ordered all the carpets for the bungalow and all the curtains with pelmets in heavy brocade material, along with a beautiful mahogany coffee table. The carpet was of top quality, in twenty-seven inch widths, which would be heat seamed together. Sheila and I were very pleased as we had ordered all the carpets with curtains for the bungalow at a fixed price and for a deposit of just one hundred pounds.

The bungalow was now finished and ready for occupation. We decided to call it 'Marralomeda'. which is an Aboriginal Australian word meaning 'best place on Earth'. Waring and Gillow sent a lorry with two men and they stayed a week, fitting all the carpets and curtains. Locally, there was uproar from the residents; the bungalow was too big, too modern. They had not realised what they had passed. It was a very unusual design and we were very pleased with it.

The locals made our lives hell for a few months, until suddenly something happened.

When we lived in Essex I had had three gnomes, each three feet high and made in concrete with steel rods. My garden at Polperro had been landscaped by professionals. I had a waterfall put in and the three gnomes were concreted into the garden.

Then one morning Sheila and I were having breakfast when the phone rang. 'Mr Bishop, your gnomes are in the river outside Nelsons Restaurant and they have a notice tied to their necks.' I went down the road and they were there. The notices read 'No development wanted in Cornwall. We don't want you here; get back to where you came from.' I rang Heinz and asked him to bring our little truck down with two men. They turned up, and with the aid of ropes, we got them into the truck and put them back in the garden.

About two hours later the local paper rang up. 'I understand the gnomes in your garden are in the river at Saxton Bridge with unpleasant notices around their necks,' said the reporter. I told him that I was looking out of my kitchen window and the gnomes were still in the garden where they had been put, so nothing could be said. Then the *Western Morning News* rang up so I said the same. I realised I had been set up, so we decided to say nothing. It was no lie that they were still in the garden.

The following day there was a knock on the door and a man was standing at the door who said he was the chairman of the local council and he had come to apologise on behalf of the local people of Polperro for what had happened to my gnomes. 'This is not the sort of thing the people do,' he said. I said, 'Thank you for the apology. We have built a lovely bungalow and we would only move out if we wanted to. We are ordinary people and we wish to help and be part of the community.'

Our daughter Karen had decided not to move down to Polperro but to stay with my mother and father in Romford to finish her education, but she came down to see us when the summer term finished and decided she would now like to move to Polperro. Grandma and Grandad were not mum and dad. Karen went to school in Looe and fitted in quite well.

I was approached by the local rowing club and asked if I would be their chairman. I was amazed, and said I knew nothing about rowing. They said I was just the right person for them and there would be no arguments as I knew nothing about rowing. I accepted, and shortly after I was approached by the British Legion in Polperro, asking if I would look into the running of the club. I was horrified to discover that they were £15,000 overdrawn at the bank, the bar was losing money and the fruit machines were not making a profit. I agreed I would become treasurer with Sheila as my assistant. The conditions I made were no committee interference and no money could be paid out except by me. Sheila and I would empty the fruit machine and bank the money directly. They all agreed and after six months we had cleared the overdraft and were back in credit. I was known as the Iron Chancellor, and ran the Legion like it was my own business.

Karen got interested in the Legion and became Polperro British Legion Queen and Miss British Legion South West. We went to Plymouth to march in with the local flag. My wife and I became interested and for several years I did the Remembrance Day parade and the lowering of the flag.

One day I went down to the harbour to find all the local fishermen leaning on the wall. One of them, who lived above us, said he was retiring and was going to sell his boat. I asked how much he was asking for her, and he said £750. On the spur of the moment, I said I would buy her. I went to tell my wife that I had bought a 23ft fishing boat with a cabin and 14 hp diesel engine. She was flabbergasted. 'What do you know about boats?' she said.

'Nothing!' I said, but I assured her I would learn.

I went the next day to look at the boat and paid the money to the fisherman. He took me on board to show me how to start the boat and steer. Nothing to it, I thought! The following day I went down

Marrelomeda at Polperro

to the harbour and all the old fishermen were leaning on the railings and telling me that I should stop just looking at it and take it out.

I climbed onto the boat and by now I was sweating. I started the engine and looked at the control panel. By now I had a number of onlookers watching and waiting. I put the boat in reverse and slowly backed out of the harbour and out into the open sea. As I was going out, they began to clap.

I decided to go to Fowey. It was quite choppy and I was making good progress until the steering wheel came off in my hands. I was panicking, as the boat was still going quite fast. I thought I should send a distress flare up, but what a laugh that would have been. Then it dawned on me that I could steer the boat by using the rudder. I slowed the boat down and crept into Polperro Harbour and moored up to the quay. Then I heard a voice shout 'what ya done to me boat?' It was the fisherman I had bought the boat from. I told him that the wheel had come off in my hands. He climbed on board muttering and wound the ropes back onto the wheel. Starting the engine he said 'We will now go forward,' but actually we went aft, banging into the quay, as he had put the ropes on back to front!

I kept the boat for about three years, and my son-in-law Richard looked after it. The keel had to be painted every year with anti-fouling paint, which was a back-aching job. The seagulls kept pooping all over it and I felt ill every time we went out, so I sold it, and that was the end of my fishing days.

CHAPTER 8

# A trip to Kenya

I was approached by Peter Minards, the Headmaster of Looe Secondary School, who lived in Polperro and ran the local greengrocer's shop. He asked if I would like to go with three teachers to Kenya on holiday. My wife refused point blank as she did not want to go, but much to her disgust, I said I would like to go. It was for twenty-eight days and I said to Peter 'If you do all the arrangements, I'll come down with my suitcase on the day and you can tell me where we're going'.

I had my passport and all the injections I needed and I had met my companions for the trip (Peter, Margaret and Vine). The plane was a Boeing 747 and after a long journey we arrived at Nairobi Airport, in hurricane force wind and rain. In the taxi to the hotel the rain nearly swept us off the road. We arrived at the hotel complex Pan Africa, a modern hotel with nice rooms.

The next morning everywhere was wet. We were picked up by our guide Sam in a camper-style truck. Sam was asked to show us the scenery, and we got stuck in the mud. We all piled out to push the van. I had a cream safari suit on and I was right behind the rear wheel, so I was splattered with mud from top to bottom. Everybody laughed till they cried. 'Never mind,' Vine said, 'When we get to Pan Africa I'll wash and press it for you.'

We got back to the Pan Africa Hotel and changed for dinner. All the meals were super. The food we had included fruit cocktail, sardine salad, consommé Julienna, roast leg of lamb, lemon meringue pie, strawberry mousse and coffee.

The next morning we were picked up by Sam again and after collecting the park ranger, we drove into the bush. Fifteen minutes later we came across six lions eating three large buffaloes. It was a bloody sight, but I filmed it on my movie camera. We then drove to the Kenyan/Tanzanian border, where we saw a sausage tree with large 'sausages,' about six inches long, hanging from them. We were quickly surrounded by a horde of children; we gave them a lot of sweets that we had brought with us. Peter (holding baby Rosie) and I had our photo taken by the sausage tree. We then drove through the bush, which scraped the side of the truck, nearly striking our faces. We saw a herd of elephants drinking in the river and my favourite animal, a giraffe, which kept peeping at us over the trees and shrubs.

We drove back to the lodge, where we had a delicious meal and retired exhausted to bed. After breakfast we left for a game ride into the park, picked up the ranger and drove towards the river. We got out and walked along the river bank towards the hippo pool, where we counted about thirty hippos wallowing in the mud, cooling off because of the heat. The highlight of the day was Vine leaping up and down shouting 'I've been stung! I've been stung again!' An insect had become trapped between Vine and her dress. Peter jumped forward, put his hand between her breasts and grabbed the insect. I filmed the whole episode. Vine was treated by Margaret, who had brought her first aid kit with her.

The next few days went quickly. We drove into the bush every day and saw lots of wild animals, including about two thousand wildebeest on one side of the river, and came across about forty elephants. Leading them was a massive elephant. We stopped the truck and they kept walking towards us, and stopped about sixteen feet away. My heart was thumping quite loud and we could see them looking at us with their big eyes. Suddenly the lead elephant lifted her trunk, snorted and led the herd away from us. That was a narrow escape.

During our trip we saw a great variety of birds, but it would take too long to describe them in this book. We saw hyenas gathering all the animal remains left by the lions. We went to Lake Nakuru where there was a hide and we saw pelicans in their hundreds. When I saw my first reebok, I turned to Peter and said 'Look there's a donkey!' Pete nearly choked laughing. We then had a long drive back to Nairobi, calling in to the Namanga Hotel for lunch and strolling around their sub-tropical gardens. In the grounds was a shop and all the local traders selling their wares. Peter and I bought a wooden carving of a Masai warrior which was about two feet tall.

It was a very rough ride; the rain was falling so hard that you could not see the road. Deep channels were carved out of the road, and if it had not been for Sam's superb driving on the firmer parts of the road we would have overturned.

We had been driving for over five hours when we came across a cluster of domed buildings made from dung. I said jokingly to Peter 'I suppose that's where we're staying'. He replied, 'Yes mate, it is!' The rest of us were quite glum.

When we approached the lodges over a road of volcanic ash, we received a wonderful welcome from the staff. Then we were shown to our lodges, which were absolutely beautiful inside; better than the hotel. There was a luxury bathroom and it was very comfortable. The lodges were grouped around a centre courtyard and we considered this construction one of the finest examples of the outdoors being brought into a living area. We had our lunch on a table where we could see water and coloured fish swimming about.

Peter and I had been invited by Nahashen to visit a Masai village and meet his father, the chief. It was very hot and we had to walk about half a mile over a rough road, with large volcanic boulders and a small opening through which people and animals could walk, to the Manyatta Compound. Nahashen took us to the chief's hut, his first wife's hut on the left and other wives in order. The huts were made from wooden frames covered with cow dung. They had very low entrances, so you had to duck to go in.

There was a pile of cow hides on the floor and we were invited to sit down in front of the chief. Peter and I were still wary in case we said something wrong and we could not make it out of the hut. We were given a cup of drink, which was goats' blood and milk. We thought about what we should do, which was to drink it of course, smiling! After two hours we thanked him for his kindness in inviting us into his hut, then presented him with some gifts, cigarettes and money and left. We arrived back at our lodge just in time for tea.

We were next taken to an area where there had been sightings of a number of lions. We arrived to find that to our horror, there were three more vehicles. We could not see lions at first, but then we spotted them in the distance. The vehicles charged through the scrub to get closer and everyone, including all of us, got out of the trucks to get a closer look. The rangers were beating the bush to stop the lions charging us, and they ordered us back into the truck. We did not know what a narrow escape we had had from an attack. One of the trucks broke down and we had to tow them out of the bush.

On the way back we came around a corner to find a large black rhino in front of us. We stopped and after ten minutes looking at us he walked off and we continued our drive back to the lodges. What an exciting day!

In the room where we had our dinner, there were three big glass doors and when it was dark, the noise of the crickets and all sorts of other insects was awesome. We left all the friends we had made and made our trip back to the Pan Africa Hotel in Nairobi. After lunch at the Stanley Hotel in Nairobi, we all separated to do some shopping. I always liked wood carvings and in a craft shop I saw three carvings of the three tribes of Kenya. They were about five feet six inches tall and were priced at £275 each. They had been carved by the second-best carver in Kenya. After a lot of bargaining, I got them down to £150 each without haulage. I met up with Peter, and on a stall I saw a three-legged stool. I sat down on it and fell over, as one leg broke off. The young man who was selling it was jumping up and down like a hyena. To pacify him I agreed to buy the stool if it was repaired and said I would collect it the next day. We were picked up from the hotel by a large African lady called Charity who took us to a purpose-built hut where we were entertained for two hours of African tribal dances; most of the dancers were topless, so it was quite fascinating!

The following day we were driving through fields of bushes which were about five feet high and covered in pineapples. We stopped and bought ten pineapples for thirty pence. Peter had a knife, so he cut them up and the five of us ate the lot. Delicious!

The road continued over the Rift Valley, a breathtaking sight. Further on we slowed down to pass through a small village, where two African girls, about fourteen or fifteen years old stepped in front of the van and asked in English if we would like our photo taken with them. We would have to pay five Kenyan shillings. While we were considering this, a large crowd of Africans arrived with a small child with open sores on his face. Peter got out his first aid kit and smeared the sores with Germolene and applied plasters. They all clapped and we got our photos for free.

We arrived at the Meru National Park. These thatched lodges were beautifully furnished with built-in showers and beds with mosquito nets. For the next few days we toured all over the park and saw every animal we could think of. Next morning we made our way to the Outspan Hotel, where we received a warm welcome and the food was excellent. The staff all waved us off and we were taken to see a huge baobab tree. The hollow centre was large enough to allow six poachers to camp inside with a fire. We spent the day chasing giraffes, lions, buffalo, wildebeest and elephants, then headed back to the hotel for a delicious dinner of egg mayonnaise, lake fish, Longonot turkey, potatoes and carrots followed by strawberry flan and coffee. After dinner we were picked up and taken to the Aldeal Bar and were entertained by the owner, a Mr Buta, a man who had been to England several times. We got back to Outspan about 11.45pm.

Next morning we spent our leisure time taking photos and cooling in the pool. The afternoon was spent watching the Kiku dancers; the Chief took a fancy to Margaret and, at the end of the dance, would not let her go. We were ready to leave her there when he finally released her and they danced a tribal dance.

Next day we headed off to Thompson Falls, and on the way we stopped to visit the Baden Powell Church and grave. We had a long walk to get to the falls, which were three hundred metres high. The noise was terrific. The lodges were very English in style, but very nice inside. We had been spoilt by all the other different lodges.

This was our last day in Kenya, the most exciting holiday I had ever experienced. We flew home the next day and were picked up by Sam for the last time to get to the airport for 9.15 pm. Leaving for the airport we had to call at a petrol station to refuel, and the toilets were most unsuitable for the ladies, who remained cross legged for the rest of the journey. We gave Sam, our courier, and all the helpers a large tip and all our Kenyan money.

There was a tropical storm and torrential rain across the road, so we had to slow to 5 miles an hour. We could not see a thing and it was very frightening. Suddenly the storm abated and we were at the airport. After we cleared customs, we were further delayed for two hours by another tropical storm. After a long journey we touched down in Rome before stopping again in Zurich and finally landing at Heathrow at 9.30 am.

We passed quickly through customs, then caught a train to Reading and changed to a train for Liskeard, where we arrived at 6.30pm. We were picked up, and Peter and I made our way back to Polperro. Sheila was pleased to see me. I climbed into bed tired out. I got up at 11 am the next morning and starting getting back to reality again.

Later that year, I came home from the office one day and Sheila said there were three huge boxes that looked like coffins sitting in the garage. I went downstairs and opened the boxes to reveal my African carvings and a note to pay £900 import tax to the Government. I quivered all over. I could not pay that sort of money. I went to see Peter Minards, who laughed and said it was 900 Kenyan pounds, which was only about 290 GB pounds. What a relief!

## CHAPTER 9

# Trenython and Fontana

Sheila had looked after our building firm, and we were now completing over seventy houses and bungalows a year. In order to do this I had an overdraft of over £150,000. One day we were in the office and I was contacted by the bank manager. He said 'I have some bad news.' The bank wanted the overdraft of £150,000 to be paid back within 14 days due to the building crisis in the country. I was shocked and explained that there was no way we could pay the money back. I demanded a meeting with the area manager in Plymouth. We were met by a very nice gentleman who had arranged a dinner for us; white tablecloth, serviettes.

After the dinner he asked how he could help us overcome the problem. I took a deep breath and said I would need another £75,000 to keep the company afloat and in exchange they could mortgage everything we owned except our hearts. My wife and I would take no salary for six months. We would keep our entire workforce and would put a property for sale at cost price to inject some cashflow into the company. He looked at us for about sixty seconds and said yes, the bank would loan us £75,000 for 12 months. We thanked him very much and went home, saved by the bank.

We met the sub-contractors and explained the situation, and they agreed to work for us. We were quite lucky and managed to sell two bungalows and two houses fairly quickly. After six months the crisis was over, and while most of the other building firms had gone into liquidation, we had ten properties for sale, so we sold them and paid back the bank. We had site agents and foremen to build our target of one hundred properties a year, but we did not need to do this, so we decided to get rid of the agents and foreman and build fifteen properties a year. My wife and I would supervise the site twice a day. After a year we found we were making more profit, with a much better life and no bank problems. What a relief.

The company had been going a few years with a good reputation, but one day I went on to my Polperro site (called Claremont Falls) and a painter who was working for me said I would love a house he was working on in Tywardreath at Par. He described it to me and it unsettled my thoughts. About three weeks later he said the owners, Mr and Mrs Crowther, had gone broke and he was owed £1500 for painting. After some haggling he got his money, but my thoughts were disturbed and I must confess that I had never heard of Tywardreath. I decided, without telling my family, to look at it.

As I always drove a Jaguar, I could not go anywhere without being recognised, so I borrowed the painter's car and drove it to Tywardreath. When I came off the Fowey road and turned towards Tywardreath, the views over the countryside were breathtaking. I suddenly saw a sign for Trenython. I drove between two large granite posts up a drive with camellia shrubs on both sides, and the house loomed into view.

I was so excited I nearly hit my head on the windscreen. It had four huge pillars with a porch. I opened the nine-foot-high entrance doors and stepped into the outer foyer. I then opened a tracery door and stepped into the main foyer, which was thirty-eight feet high in the centre with a glass roof. I turned around and saw a beautiful mahogany staircase in the centre of the room branching off left and right and leading to a six-foot hallway with ten apartments leading off. The doors were eight feet high and three feet wide and made of polished mahogany; the feel of them made my heart flutter.

I looked into one of the apartments, which had views over the River Fowey to Par Docks. Downstairs there was a ballroom, a bar and an eating area and on the left side was the restaurant; a room completely panelled with carved panels brought from various churches, including Yorkminster. Beyond that there was the kitchen leading to a swimming pool which was under construction, so it was blockwork only with no windows or roof, just half built.

I came away very excited and wondering how I was going to persuade the family to let me buy it. I went home and said to my wife and Karen, 'I have just looked at a house of the sort that I have always wanted to own. I want to show you.' They jumped into the car and I took them to Tywardreath, and as we drove between the granite outposts and along the bumpy drive, they suddenly saw the house. With horror on their faces they said, 'don't be ridiculous, how could we run a place like this?'

I looked at them and said 'now, if you drive a Mini and then we drive a Rolls Royce it looks huge, so you have to look at the house in this context. What an exciting adventure it would be to have this challenge.'

I attended the auction to buy it and bid £350,000, my limit, but I was outbid by £5000. I went home disappointed, but Sheila said that the man who had bought Trenython was not capable of running it and it would be up for sale within the year. I asked her how she knew, as she wasn't at the auction. She just said to wait and see, and about six months later the owner rang me and asked if I was interested in buying it. He wanted twice what he paid for it, so I said I was not interested. I did go down to Trenython and found that he had painted the outside columns pink! When I went inside it was like a morgue. I thought what a poor old house it now was, and went home. Sheila said we would get the house in the end.

About three months later Trenython went into receivership and I offered £350,000 to the receivers, which was accepted. I was able to purchase it with no mortgage. My daughter sold her bungalow in Polperro and we all moved into Trenython. I decided to keep my house in Polperro in case we had to move back.

Trenython was built in 1872 for Colonel Peard, who fought in Italy with Garibaldi. He was knighted over there and was called Garibaldi's Englishman, and Garibaldi commissioned an Italian architect to design

Trenython the home of the Lord Bishop of Truro

and build the house. As well as the magnificent staircase, the outside stonework was superb; I put a level to it and it was spot on. The third owner of Trenython was Bishop Gott, who was appointed Bishop of Truro. He did not like his quarters in Truro and, as he was quite a wealthy man, he bought the house and it became known as Bishops Palace. The Bishop who came brought all the carved wood panelling with him, and this was what was installed in the restaurant. In 1925, Trenython became a Railway Convalescent Home.

Here we were living in a house with ten apartments, a restaurant, bar and a half-built swimming pool plus seven lodges built for time-share in thirty acres; how the hell were we going to run it? Karen

The Terrace of the Railway Convalescent home Trenython

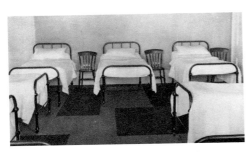

The Metropolitan Ward, Trenython

The Lounge. The Railway Convalescent home, Trenython

was going to run the restaurant and visitors. Richard was going to look after the bar and maintenance, Sheila was going to look after the accounts, and I was going to put Trenython on the map. The house was built at the end of a long drive and local people found it intimidating, so I decided our meal prices would be 5% lower than other restaurants and the bar prices the same as pub prices. I then looked around to find a chef and poached one called Dennis Ackers from the Carlyon Bay Hotel. I explained what I wanted from the kitchen and gave him a free hand. Very soon we were doing 70 Sunday lunches at £5.50 a head. The bar was used by locals and we sold the beer they liked.

The local car club had their annual dinner at Trenython Manor and Colin Vincent, who had a motor museum, said he was retiring. I asked him if he would mind if I tried to build one, and he said fine. I started to look for a site. I managed to find a twenty-five-acre site at Par Moor in Cornwall. I paid ECP £250,000 for the site and engaged an architect to draw the plans from my sketches. It was an eye-catching design with a 54,000 square foot museum, a restaurant, a fast food café and a conference centre.

The plans were passed by Cornwall Council and I placed contracts to build the museum for over £500,000. The foundations were piled to a depth of 100 feet. All went well and I placed a contract for £350,000 for all the steel frame structures. I managed to pay for the steel frame, but I had run out of money. I tried to borrow a million pounds from the bank, but they refused. I wrote to Bernie Ecclestone offering a 50% interest in the building. I received a nice letter back but no money. With the costs climbing to £475,000, I had no option but to stop the building of the museum. At the time I had bought, over the three-year period, twenty-five classic cars for the museum which I had stored in a small factory unit in Par. The lady who owned the unit gave me one months' notice to vacate the factory after three years' occupation, so I had to sell 16 vehicles below cost to get them moved quickly. I moved the most valued ones to my garage at home.

I was in a fix, but suddenly we had an offer for £950,000 for half the site from a company who were going to build a large holiday complex at Carlyon Bay in St. Austell. I had no option but to sell half the site to them and clear all my debts so I had money in the bank. Alas, the museum project was doomed. It was the only project I had not completed in my life. I still own twelve and a half acres at the site.

When I closed my building business I kept on three men who had worked for over twenty years at Trenython. They finished off the swimming pool in blue mosaic and built a sauna and jacuzzi. I decided to have the outside of the house painted and found it would cost more than £10,000 for scaffolding, which we could not afford,

The cherry picker for painting Trenython

so I hired a cherry picker for a month for £600. When it arrived we extended the arm and my son in law and the painter looked at it, and with their faces ashen grey, said they couldn't go up there. I said 'Of course you can, I'll show you!' I went up in the box piece, up to the top windows, safety rail all around. I came down and after some discussion and the promise of a bonus they agreed to paint Trenython. The best bit was the bell tower. The cherry picker was not long enough at full extension, so Richard tied a broom on the end and was able to paint the clock tower.

We then started to do weddings, so to make sure they went smoothly I supervised the proceedings, dressed in my dinner suit with a bow tie. I introduced the bride, the groom and best man. I was always nervous and my mind would go blank, so I wrote the names of the bride and groom on the palms of my hands. The dining room was done out in gold and white and I bought a silver cake stand and knife. I'm not boasting but the layout always looked superb. We did over two hundred weddings at Trenython, with the help of Karen, who supervised all the meals. It was no easy job getting them out quickly. We had a file full of letters of praise. The turnover was reaching £400,000 when Sheila became very ill; she lost the use of one eye and was in a wheelchair.

We found we needed to spend about £120,000 on the roof, which we did not have, so I decided we would have to sell up. I felt we would still like to live here so I cut off 14 acres of land from Trenython and designed a house on it, catering for Sheila's needs. It had no steps, wide doors, and a large bedroom with an ensuite bathroom. It took two years to get planning after a lot of hassle with the council, and it was a further eighteen months before we could move in. At that point I put Trenython up for sale. We sold to an Arab family for £850,000, but we kept the stable block and the two semi-detached houses that had been built in the 1930s for the railway workers.

At Trenython there were six wrought iron lanterns, about three feet long, and it was said that they had come from one of the palaces in Rome. They were valued at about £25,000 each. I went in one day to find that they had been removed. I told the owner he couldn't take them out, but the owner said it was not a listed house so they could do as they liked. I thought, is that so! I went home and I spoke to a friend of mine and got Trenython listed in four weeks. I then went back to Trenython and told them that they could not remove anything else. They had to concede defeat, and after two years, they sold the place to a Spanish consortium, Calle CLS. They wanted to buy the houses and stable block and I managed to get £150,000 for them. I had sold Trenython for a million pounds and built a beautiful house in the 14 acres I had kept.

Fontana was the new house I lived in with Sheila, and I designed and built it with the aid of my son-in-law and three men who had been in our employ for the last fifteen years. It was on a sloping site set in 14 acres of garden and forest. How lucky to be able to look out of all the windows at the front of the house to have a view over rolling fields towards the expanse of water and the coast line of Pentewan

Sands in the background. The view extended across St Austell Bay to Par and the slopes opposite, where the inlet to Mevagissey lies. This is the most wonderful view, and it changes every day; dense mist in the morning, followed by the sun (it is so bright in the kitchen I often have to pull the blind down). Later, by the evening, we can view the sunset flickering before going down on the horizon. At night time I can also see the lights of St Austell twinkling through the massive fir trees which are on our boundary. I often see the large commercial boats being guided by tugs into Par harbour to load the china clay which is exported all over the world by Imerys, the French company that acquired China Clay ECC Ltd. The china clay is produced by extracting it at high water pressure from the granite in the clay pits about five miles away and transported by lorry to Par Docks.

The garden is set in a valley and I have constructed an Italian styled central section with fountains, statues and waterfalls. There are 150 acer trees which are under planted with thousands of blue-bells and primroses in spring time. When you look in the lower half of the garden looking at the mass of bluebells with no music, no phones, no cars and no people, you are in a magical world. In the garden are bamboos that are three inches in diameter and twenty feet tall, surrounded by tree ferns, the giant rhubarb *Gunnera manicata*, handerkerchief trees, eucalyptus, the fire tree, camellias some 15 feet tall, rhododendrons, and chusan palm trees some 20 feet high. I have built a tree house in the garden shaped like a church with a wooden staircase leading to it.

Excavating the slope

When I started on the construction of Fontana's gardens the site was a mass of brambles and trees that had fallen down, and in order to get down the steep slope to start work, my digger driver, Wesley, had to excavate the slope until we could walk down. I knew I wanted an Italian garden and I had placed an order with my friend John Sweet from Par Garden Centre. Included in that order was a huge Italian fountain and 12 full-size statues made from marble dust and cement at a cost of £12,500. If they were real marble they would have cost thousands of pounds. I also wanted a waterfall seventy feet high and I was lucky enough to have a friend who worked for English China

Installing the Italian Fountain

My Grandson Robert beside a load of granite for the waterfall

Ben transporting some of the granite boulders

Clay and was able to obtain one hundred tons of granite boulders, which they gave me, but I had to pay for cartage. Wesley dug a big pit at the top of the garden and the lorries tipped them into the pit. The noise was tremendous. Each piece weighed over two hundredweight and they had to be picked up by the machine, with chains around them, and taken down the garden, swinging around, and placed where I wanted them. It was a slow job, but the effect today is breathtaking.

New trees were planted. One and a half acres in the centre of the garden was a bog and when you stepped on it your feet disappeared into the mud. This was drained with a series of pipes into a stream in the side of the garden, and we planted some giant rhubarb.

The Cana Gunnera we planted

We decided to cut down a number of dead trees to give the house a better view, and we also cleared the brambles and cleared up the trees that had fallen down over the last 40 years. I hired Mark, Duggie and Brian, my loyal band of workers, with their small track digger to carry out the project. In order for the digger to operate you have to

cut a track through the undergrowth, as it would topple over if you tried to go up the slope and down. After three weeks all the dangerous trees had been taken down the view from my kitchen table, where I am writing this, is wonderful. As I look out of the window I first see all the trees and shrubs I have planted over the last twenty years and then there are fields sloping away with sheep and cattle.

We had been working on the garden for about four weeks and I was in the front of my house talking to my daughter when a man in a dark suit came up to me and asked if I was the owner of Fontana. I said I was and asked who he was. 'I am the Chief Enforcement Officer for the Council, and it has been reported to us [by some busybody] that you are cutting trees down and using a digging machine. I wish to go down the garden and check.'

I asked him if he had a warrant, which he duly produced. I then took him down the garden and he said there was a preservation order on the trees. I told him that it was news to me! He then produced some plans dated 1978. We had bought the land in 1999, with no mention of tree orders, but I said 'You can see we are only clearing brambles, bracken and dead trees, some having been down more than forty years. The only trees we've cut down have been diseased or damaged.' He replied that I could not cut into the soil more than twelve inches (30cm).

I said 'Use your common sense, you have to cut a platform for a machine to operate or it would topple over.'

He then said, 'I want you to stop work immediately, you are committing a criminal offence.'

I pointed out how it might not look good if a man approaching 80 went to jail for landscaping a garden. He did not appreciate my humour. He took some photos and said he would get the council's tree expert to see if we had broken the law on tree cutting. This was on a Wednesday, and after four days I had not received any letters from the council, so we proceeded with the landscaping of the steep slopes.

## CHAPTER 10

# A tragedy, and a trip down memory lane

❖ ❖

It is Saturday 29th December 2007, and I am still waiting to receive my passport because the authorities lost my particulars from 28 years ago and I have had to send my birth certificate. I need a passport so that I can go to France to have a knee operation.

It is now five months since I lost Sheila, on July 27th. She had been admitted to hospital with a ruptured ulcer, but she contracted the Clostridium difficile (C. Diff.) bug, which destroyed her bowel function and affected her muscles. I decided to care for her at home with the aid of a special bed, a hoist and a wheelchair. Two carers came in morning and evening, and I fed Sheila and cared for her each day, until one morning I woke up and knew she had gone.

I kissed her for the last time with tears running down my cheeks. After 53 years of marriage, I was on my own. Although I needed a knee operation I could not trust myself to go into any hospital in Cornwall.

The doctor said Sheila had all the symptoms of motor neurone disease. I had her cremated because of the way she had suffered in the last six months of her life. There were no flowers except for a magnificent arrangement of red roses on her coffin; these were the type of flowers she had when we got married. The mourners donated £1500 to Mount Edgcumbe Hospice for cancer patients.

Now I sit on the chair in the kitchen where she sat and look at the wedding photo opposite me. I shed tears every day when I think of her. A part of me has gone forever.

One morning in 2012 I was reading the *Western Morning News* and saw a competition to win a seven-day holiday in Canada. It explained that the person who collected the most coupons in the next month would win. I went down to the newsagents and bought fifteen copies. Keith, the owner, asked what was going on and I showed him the paper. He rubbed his hands and asked how many more copies I would want. I ordered twenty-five copies for four days. It made my hand ache cutting out the coupons. I now had one hundred and fifteen coupons and had spent over one hundred pounds. I decided over the week to buy further copies, which gave me 235 coupons, which I posted off.

About two weeks later the phone rang and I was told that I had won the competition and the prize was a seven-day all-inclusive holiday to Canada with flights for two people. I thought that as I had no one to go with, I would have to raffle it for charity as it was unfair to ask just one family member to accompany me. Then my granddaughter Anna-Louise said she would like to go, and the family got together and agreed she should.

We caught a flight to Montreal on a Boeing 747 and on arrival were taken to the Sheraton Hotel. We had a lovely room with a view and two double beds. The hotel had an indoor garden with a waterfall spanning three floors and an escalator with mirror walls. The food was excellent. The next day we explored Montreal. We saw the famous tower, and when we got back to the hotel we asked reception if we could book a meal in the tower restaurant. She said it was full. We explained to her how we had come to be on this holiday and that we would be speaking to the newspaper about our experiences. She phoned again and got us booked in the restaurant. It was very exciting; it took twenty-five seconds to reach the top of the tower and we got out on to a glass floor which you could look down through. A lot of people were too nervous to stand on it.

We had a lovely holiday and got on like a house on fire. My grand-daughter liked to shop, and she suddenly stopped to look at some shoes in the window; they were priced at £60. I said they were far too expensive and we carried on walking. Then I spotted a beautiful red silk tie with silver spots in the pattern. I love ties, so we went into the shop and I asked the price and nearly had a heart attack when I heard it was £45! I said I would think about it.

The next morning we were coming to the end of the holiday, so I thought, why not? We went back to the shoe shop and bought the shoes and to the tie shop and bought the tie and handkerchief. I have worn the tie on many occasions and the comments I have had from everyone proved it was worth every penny.

The next day we said goodbye to everyone and boarded the plane home. We arrived at Heathrow and caught the coach back to Cornwall after a wonderful holiday.

On another occasion, I saw an offer in our local paper for tickets to the Grand Design Exhibition at the Excel Centre in London. I phoned my Friend Nick Witcombe and the two of us booked two rooms at the Travelodge by the City Airport. Nick picked me up at 12 o'clock on Tuesday 7th May 2013. We purred our way to the hotel in his BMW. As we got closer to London I said to Nick that we were 10 miles from Romford, where I was born. He said on the spur of the moment that he would drive me there. A feeling welled up inside me, the excitement of going back after 81 years to the house I was born in.

We came to Romford to see that the whole landscape had altered with new roads and buildings. We drove down Pettits Lane and I directed Nick to the third turning on the left, which was Woodlands Road. We slowly drove into Woodlands Road and came to number 22: my birthplace. I got out of the car, remembering walking to school during the war and picking up the bullets, shrapnel and aircraft debris in the gutters after the nightly raids by the Germans on London. I knocked on the door and a gentleman in his sixties opened the door and I told him I was born in this house 81 years ago. The man gasped and went to fetch his wife. I told them that the leaded window in their front door had been made by me in 1951. In order to protect it they had put a piece of glass on both sides. They invited me in and I showed them the bedroom I was born in. I said my parents had bought this house in 1938 for £795 and similar houses were now selling for £300,000 or more.

After shaking hands with them we then drove to Gidea Park, where I saw the house we had built for my parents. It was built using bricks called Autumn Tints and it looked the same as when we had built it except for additions. Next door stood the family glass business, John Bishop and Son, started by my father in 1928. It was now called Bishop Glass, but it was closed.

We then drove on to Havering-atte-Bowe where we had lived before moving to Cornwall. The house was completely derelict, having been unoccupied for a number of years. When we had moved to Cornwall we had sold the house for £26,500; it sold recently for £1.5 million. Now surrounded by a number of cameras, the house was protected like Fort Knox. Unfortunately no one was at home, so we were only able to walk around the outside. Bedfords Park next door, the cricket ground and the village green all looked the same.

As the time was going on, we went through Ilford and Stratford and arrived at the Travelodge at 7.30 pm. The car parking was £7.50 for 24 hours, which was very reasonable. Nick and I each had a room, and they were very nice and clean and had everything we needed. After settling, we were going out to dinner, but decided to eat in the hotel restaurant. We both had starters and when I ordered I explained to the waiter (who was of Pakistani origin) that when I go out I like to try something new. I said 'If I have the curry, I won't get wonky eyes?' He looked at me and smiled, and said, 'I eat curry every day. It is delicious – look at the glow on my face.'

I enjoyed the curry, and the total cost of the meal for two was great value at £28. The lager was 68p cheaper than in Cornwall. We were right by the side of the City Airport and the planes were taking off every four minutes.

The next morning we had a full English breakfast and then checked out and went to find the Excel Exhibition Centre, which was on the right bank of the River Thames. We were both amazed at how clear the water was. The Excel centre has a modern design and is surrounded by hotels. The design literally takes your breath away. I was a bit disappointed with the exhibition, which was called Grand Designs, but there were no houses or plans of anything outstanding. We were looking for a design for a house for a site in Cornwall with a 45-degree slope. The exhibits were kitchens, bathrooms, windows etc. We got to the exhibition at about 1030 am and left at 2 pm.

As we started on our journey home Nick asked if I would like to go to Shenfield, where Sheila and I had self-built our bungalow. I told him that would be wonderful and it would be the icing on the cake. We had to go through Romford, and as we were passing Bishop Glass we noticed it was now open. We pulled into the forecourt and walked down the side of the shop to the factory. It was like a time warp, as the factory was exactly as I had built it in 1958.

A man came towards us and I said 'My name is Bishop, and I am the original owner'. He shook my hand and called another man, who was the current owner. I said to him that he was using the original glass bench and glass racks that I had built in the 1960s. When we owned the glass business we had employed fifteen staff and had three lorries. Sadly, due to health and safety regulations, these businesses were not able to secure contracts from the large contractors and only employed three staff and had one van. When I ran the business we imported glass from Belgium, Germany and Czechoslovakia.

As we were leaving the works the man in my parents' house smiled and spoke. I told him I had built the house in 1960 and he was delighted to hear about it. He said that perhaps I could help him to explain why he kept digging up bricks like part of a wall. I said to him that when my father had bought the land the previous owners had put in the foundations for five shops, but the firm went bankrupt. The bricks that were being dug up were the remains of that building work.

We then made our way to Shenfield, going through Brentwood. Alas the Odeon Cinema where Sheila and I used to go on a Saturday was no longer there. Shenfield had been a village when we lived there, but was now all built up and very busy. I said to Nick 'take the next left turning, Hanging Hill Lane, then take the third turning on the left at Hall Green Lane.' My heart was beating fast as we got close to the bungalow Sheila and I had built when we were getting married. Round the next bend there was a bungalow on the corner of Shelby Road. I gasped – they had built two houses in the back garden and another on the front where the detached garage had been. All the original leaded windows I had made in 1954 were still there and the bungalow looked the same, except that they had built rooms in the roof.

To my disappointment there was nobody in, but at that moment a car drew up next door and I ran over to speak to the ladies. I said 'Excuse me, but do you know the name of the people who live in the bungalow?' I told them my wife and I had built it in 1954 for £1500 and our daughter Karen was born in the front bedroom. She was quite interested and said her husband, Maurice, would be disappointed not to have met me. We shook hands and Nick said how friendly the people in Essex had been to us. I said how exciting this had been. We then made our way back to Cornwall and arrived at 9.45pm. What an adventure!

I lived in a lovely house with a beautiful garden, but I was lonely. I was lucky to having Tristan working for me in the garden, but I had no one to talk to, so I thought I would go on some coach trips.

I was looking through the local paper, the *Western Morning News*, one Saturday morning in March 2011 and spotted an advert for a coach trip to the RHS Chelsea Flower Show; one night in a London Hotel and a visit to Kew Gardens. I suffer from travel sickness and I had not been on a coach for 35 years, but I had always wanted to go to the Chelsea show so I plucked up courage and phoned for a brochure. With a single supplement the price was £140, I decided to take a chance and booked the tour.

A friend of mine rang me the day before and said that if I took a newspaper and sat on it, it would cure me of my travel sickness. I thought it was a load of tripe, but said I would try it. On Saturday morning I got up at six o'clock as I had to pick up the coach at 7.40 outside the Wills Hotel in Liskeard. I climbed on the coach and found I was in the back seat and the middle seat was not occupied. I looked around at my fellow passengers; not a bad bunch, I thought. The people next to me spoke and I found out they had the same solicitor as me and the gentleman used to look after the Talbot cars that Anthony Blight used to own. I have a number of cars dating back to 1913, so we had something in common to talk about.

Exeter was the next stop, and here a lady got on and sat next to me in the seat against the window. She seemed quite pleasant, so I passed the time of day with her. We stopped at two motorway restaurants.

Going into London was an eye opener; traffic nose to tail and at a complete standstill. Some of the new buildings built in glass were fascinating. I am not a lover of modern architecture, but I was impressed. We arrived at Chelsea at 3.45pm, the courier got the tickets and we walked straight in past the long queue. I bought a programme for £5 and decided to look at the show gardens first. There were hundreds of people, so this was a slower process.

The gardens looked smaller than they appear on the television. Quite a lot of them were modern with glass and water running in slots cut into granite, which seemed nice but soulless. Diarmuid Gavin had a flower garden suspended on a 70-foot crane which was being lowered and raised. There were several natural gardens which you could relate to.

I was looking at the statues and saw a nice bronze statue of a woman holding another woman in her hand. I thought it would look nice in the new memorial garden I was constructing in memory of my wife Sheila, so I asked the gentleman trader how much it would cost. He replied, 'A hundred and twenty thousand pounds sir. Are you interested?' I said, 'if you build me a house to go with it, then I will say yes.' He laughed.

The next exhibit was displaying statues, lions, and a circular rotunda with a domed room in stone. I enquired the price - £25,000, but I could have a 20 per cent discount if bought at the show. I showed the lady some photos of my garden and the owner came over and after a discussion he said I could have one delivered for about £17,000. It was very reasonable, but at that moment, although I was asset rich, I had nil cash flow.

I then went to the flower marquee, which was absolutely marvellous. The quality of the plants and blooms were out of this world.

I went on several other coach outings, including seeing the Blackpool lights and going up the tower, but I was still very lonely. My daughter Karen and my three grandchildren, Anna-Louise, Mary and Robert, came to see me every week. I decorated the house at Christmas. It looked lovely, but I missed having Sheila around.

I was reading our local paper when I saw an advert for a coach tour to Windsor Castle, Buckingham Palace and the gardens. I had always wanted to see Windsor Castle and the Palace gardens, so I decided to book. I had to be in St Austell for the coach at 6.30am. Karen picked me up at 6 am and when I got on the coach at 7.15 there were three other people on board. We picked up passengers along the route and stopped off at one of the motorway complexes, where I had chicken, chips and beans. The chips were soft and soggy and the chicken was dry and tough, so I took it back and spoke to the restaurant manager, who gave me my money back.

Arriving at Windsor at 2.30 pm with pre-booked tickets we were allowed to walk straight in. What a superb castle. After the terrible fire in 1992, the main hall had been rebuilt. It was gratifying to see that thanks to the superb workmanship of today's craftsmen, the castle could look the same as the original. After coming out of the castle I took a one-hour trip on an open-top bus around Windsor and saw the wonderful architecture; it was an invigorating tour.

Then we arrived at the Bull Hotel, Gerrards Cross, about twenty-five minutes from Windsor. The Bull Hotel is a black and white building with over two hundred rooms. We were warmly welcomed and I was given the key to room 138. As a single passenger I expected a small room, but it was superb; a huge double bed, good quality furnishings, spotlessly clean, tea, coffee, everything you could wish for.

After a lovely hot shower I decided to have every meal in the restaurant. It was a very nice meal with the bread baked while the food was being prepared. The service was slow, but as I was not in a hurry I did not complain. I particularly enjoyed the palace gardens, and overall it was a very pleasant trip.

Between trips I was still running my company, and I had some land at Seaton in Cornwall which I had bought in 1973 with planning permission for eighteen bungalows. I forgot to renew the planning permission after one year and the Council refused to honour its obligations; I appealed twice, but the inspector ruled against it. In the early 80s I was approached by a consultant, who on looking at the paperwork decided that it was too complicated for him. However he knew a consultant in Devon whose expenses were £135 per hour. I approached him and he said he thought he could do something, but the council refused to budge and after eighteen months we went to appeal. The inspector ruled in our favour and we were awarded £20,000 costs. The council was furious and decided to appeal. The inspector said they would lose and he felt they had treated us badly and thought that we should go to the ombudsman.

The council knew they were on a loser and backed down, but they raised every obstacle. We engaged top award-winning architects Arco 2 to design twelve houses of a most modern design. The council refused and said we could only build ten such houses. After six months we were granted planning permission. We still had a long way to go, including a close encounter with wildlife and the planners.

The Seaton land is a beautiful hillside site just four minutes from the beach. Finally, after twenty years of hassle from the planners and a considerable legal bill, I finally received permission for twelve detached 1700 square foot houses. Now, in 2012, as I am approaching 81 I decided, with all the new planning regulations regarding building houses, I would put the roads and services in and sell the building plots for self-builders. I engaged a plant hire firm, a father and son, to clear the site and mark out the plot.

Some of the residents below the site had squatted on part of it, and I had the problem of removing them. The solicitor advised us that as we had a registered title to this land we should simply take it back. The fifteen-ton truck machine started to munch its way through the brambles and undergrowth, at which point a man came rushing up shouting at us to stop. He said 'you can't do that. It is my land!' I showed him the Land Registry plan. He said 'No, no, no, you do not own it as you have not cultivated it.' I stood in front of the machine and beckoned to the driver to move forward. The man started ranting and raving, at which point his wife came up and I showed her the plan. Her husband kept shouting and interrupting. I said 'Will you shut up while I talk to your wife?' and at this point he came forward to clout me, but his wife restrained him by standing in front of me. I said to her that if she could restrain her husband from verbally assaulting me, when I had marked out the road any land left I would let them have, but if he continued to interfere with the land clearance I would take back every square meter we owned. They agreed, and with a sigh of relief the first crisis was over and work proceeded smoothly.

Five days later I received a telephone call from the site about 4 pm from the digger driver to say they had had the local police, the planning officer, the RSPCA and a Mr Evans from half a mile away. Mr Evans had sneaked onto our site and reported us to the police for destroying a badger sett. The three men on site were given a caution from the police, but no one had informed us, the owners. I phoned the RSPCA, whose officer said he could not discuss it with me as they were going to prosecute us.

A meeting was arranged for 2 pm the next Monday. I attended with my grandson Robert. When they turned up I could not believe my eyes – we had the police, the RSPCA inspector and a special badger advisor from another county. We all trooped up the steep slope where the men were erecting a stockproof fence to keep farm animals from roaming on the site. In the back was a hole about 9 inches in diameter and for two hours the experts tried to prove it was a badgers sett, whether it was occupied and if we had destroyed it. We had previously cleared the site twice over the last four years and we had not encountered any problems before.

I produced a schedule of the various times we had cleared the site. The council had been informed and we had had two wildlife reports, with no mention of any badger setts on the land. The officials went off for a conflab and then the RSPCA pair said that they would dearly like to prosecute my company, but they felt that as there was no mention of badger setts in the wildlife report, they did not think they would secure a conviction, and also we had not intentionally damaged the sett, a claim which I had disputed on the basis that the hole was still open.

The police were very sympathetic and said a prosecutor would not succeed. They took the caution off the contractor and said that if Mr Evans trespassed on the site again they would prosecute him. A sigh of relief, another obstacle had been overcome.

We had previously cleared the site and at the last minute the council planners had stepped in and said there could be dormice on the site, so for six months we had fifty little tunnels on the site to see if any dormice went through. They were monitored every month, and at the end of the six months no dormice had been found on the site and the council had to concede defeat. This cost the company £3500 for the report.

The council then said there could be slow worms on the site. I resisted this, so it was agreed that a wildlife expert would walk in front of the excavator with a net and move any slow worms to another spot. All this happened before we had even started the clearance. I was wondering whether I would live long enough to enjoy the proceeds.

CHAPTER 11

# A new chapter

One day in 2013 I was reading our local paper and looking through the coach trips. I spotted a trip to Hampton Court Flower Show, a place I had never been in eighty-odd years. I booked over the phone for a two-day trip with a stay at a hotel near Heathrow and a trip to Windsor Castle the next day. The only problem with the trip was that I had to get on the coach at 6.15 am, so I had to ask my daughter to pick me up at 5.45.

I decided to take a packed lunch, a cheese and pickle sandwich, and bought a cup of tea which was served in a large white cup that was so heavy I needed two hands to hold it. We arrived at Hampton Court at 2.30 pm ready to go in at 3 pm. What a place, spread over thirty acres; a wonderful show and I met a lot of people. I had to be back on the coach by 7.30, but I came out of the wrong entrance and got lost. I had to walk for nearly a mile before I found the coach park, which had about forty coaches, and the temperature was in the eighties. When we had arrived at the hotel there were only five coaches in front of us.

I had a lovely room with a double bed, nicely furnished and with a nice shower. I decided to have a meal in the restaurant. What an adventure! When I asked for a table for one I was shown to a table tucked away. I sat down and the chair back was loose and the chair wobbled. I called the waiter, who apologised and brought me another chair. I looked at the menu and decided to order the special of the night. which was soup followed by pork chop, chips and salad.

After waiting about 15 minutes I saw the chef dish up the soup, then after another 10 minutes the waiter brought it to my table. I said they could take it back and bring me hot soup. The chef looked at me with evil eyes and a hot bowl of soup duly arrived. I tasted the soup and it needed more salt and pepper, but there was no salt and pepper on the table. I called the waiter, who said 'You take the salt and pepper out of this pot,' which of course was empty. He tried about six different tables before he found one that was full. In the meantime the chef was watching me intently.

I then asked the waiter for some vinegar and he brought me a whole stack of vinegar sachets. I tugged them, tried biting them but could not open them, so I called the waiter over to open them for me. The restaurant manager came over. I said 'I used to run a holi-day complex in Cornwall and the first task in the morning is to fill the salt, pepper and vinegar pots'. I told him that I had enjoyed the meal and laughed about all that had gone wrong. He said he would give me 10% discount on the meal and asked if I would like a cup of coffee on the house. I asked if I could have a weak coffee, which then arrived with no milk in it at all. I called him over, smiling and said 'sorry about this but could I have some milk?' He had to get a girl to go to another place and get the milk. I smiled at her and said that this meal had been more entertaining than going to the cinema.

It was very hot in bed, but I had brought my own pillow and fell asleep. Next morning, the Continental breakfast was at 8 am. I came down from my room and had lined up for breakfast when I was aware of two ladies standing in front of me. They turned and saw me there alone and asked me if I would like to join them for breakfast. I thought two attractive ladies? How could I not!

I looked after their handbags while they got breakfast and then joined them with a full English breakfast. We were all going to Windsor Castle, so I invited them to have lunch with me. Outside the castle as we were waiting to go in we could hear music and were lucky enough to see the Trooping of the Colour.

We had a tour of the castle. It is truly a magnificent place; we got neckache looking at the ceilings. I spoke to the guide, who said that Prince Philip had designed the circular tower section and the tiled design on the floor. I chatted to the ladies; the mother was a widow and also a keen gardener. Her name was Marina and she lived about forty-five minutes in the car from me. I invited them over to look at my garden, but whether they would come I had no idea.

I must mention our courier, Susan, who was very slender and not much of her, but she looked after us very well. She came up to me and said, 'Mr Bishop, what a smartly-dressed man you are.' I always wear a tie and highly polished shoes and put a handkerchief in my top pocket. I coughed and explained that I always dressed like this.

As we were going along Susan said her husband used to be in the Guards and often did guard duty at Windsor Castle. She said they did four hours on and two hours off. When they were off, they had to clean their uniforms and boots. The bearskin they wore had to be turned upside down, shaken in talcum powder and brushed. On guard outside the castle one winter, the Queen had stopped and said to her husband 'you must be freezing out here,' but as a guard is not able to move or speak, he only blinked his eyes in response and she blinked back and smiled.

There were so many people at the castle that we could only see the Queen's dolls house from a distance before we hurried back to the coach. It was a good journey home and Marina and her daughter waved to me and blew me a kiss. I wondered if I would see her again.

I arrived home at about 10.15 pm and my grandson Robert picked me up and took me home. The trip cost £154, which was great value for money. I was looking forward to my next adventure, which was opening my gardens to the public on 21st July 2013, in aid of the local village funds.

About three or four weeks later the phone rang. It was Marina, asking if she could come over with her daughter to look at the garden. I had not told her that the garden was 14 acres. They both arrived and firstly were astonished at the house. We went down the garden, which is set in a valley with slopes either side. I showed them around, which we all enjoyed as they were also keen gardeners. We came back to the kitchen for tea and a slice of strawberry sponge and they sat looking out of the window at the view over the gardens into St Austell Bay, the clay compound and a panoramic view over St Austell town.

I looked at Marina, who had long blonde hair, and thought how nice looking she was. We chatted and she asked me over to her bungalow in Wadebridge on Sunday. I went over there for Sunday lunch and we had a lovely time. Marina kissed me when we said goodbye and I went home very happy. I knew I had met somebody I liked.

The wind was howling and the rain beating down, but someone very precious came to wish me a happy New Year. I was on my own and I hadn't seen my family. A telephone call is not like seeing someone in the flesh. Feeling sorry for myself, I decided to do my tax return, and there was a knock on the door and to my astonishment Marina was standing there. My heart started to quicken as we embraced each other and kissed passionately. Marina had braved the wind, rain and flood and driven for 45 minutes to see me. She truly did love me.

Marina and I were working in the garden, and she said she wanted a bag of compost. I put the bag on my trolley and started to wheel it along the path when it started to run away. I put my hand out to steady myself and my hand got caught between two cast iron cockerels and crushed it. The pain was intense. Marina rushed to my aid and took me to the doctors, who sent me to Cornwall Hospital in Truro. The doctor said they could not save my finger and would have to cut it off. I asked if he was sure, but he said they couldn't save it. At 12 midnight night I watched them saw off my finger. I had to stay in hospital another day.

Marina came to pick me up and took me home. After three weeks they took the dressing off. It was healing very well, although it was only half a finger, and I still find it annoying when picking things up and shaving.

About six months later my back and legs were playing me up. The doctor had said that I should have a new hip about two years ago and did not know how I endured the pain. I asked how long I would have to wait and he said six months on the NHS and three weeks privately. I paid to have it done privately and was walking after five weeks, so it was a success.

I still had a problem walking, so I asked a consultant to look at my back. He said it was completely worn out and I had three vertebrae touching each other, which was the reason for all this pain. I said I would pay for an operation, but he said that due to my age they could not perform an operation and I would have to go home, take pain-killers, do no lifting and put up with it. That was four years ago, and I have gradually got worse and cannot walk without a four wheeled trolley. I am not a happy man, and it has curtailed my activities.

Although I had a job to walk I continued to open Fontana for Mount Edgcumbe Hospice and we have raised over £3000 over the last few years. Karen, Marina and Anna-Louise did all the cream teas, sandwiches, teas and coffees. We charged £5 for a cream tea and a tour of the garden. I could not have opened the garden to the public without Tristan, my gardener, who worked part time for me (full time now) and has been with me for twelve years.

I never went on a holiday abroad with Sheila, as she would not fly and I was seasick on boats. I was not short of money and I decided I should see some of the world. I said to Marina 'would you like to come on holiday to Canada with me?' She said she would love to.

It was a long journey and we landed in Montreal very tired, with nobody there to pick us up. I phoned the hotel and was told to make my own way to the hotel. We got there to find our courier talking to other members of the party. I was fuming and I went up to him and gave him hell. I said, 'if this is how we are going to be looked after we might as well catch the flight home.' He said to me 'why don't you both go up to your room, relax, I will see you both in the morning.'

At 9.30 the next morning, we had breakfast and the courier had a glint in his eyes as he said he hoped we had slept well. He proceeded to tell us the itinerary for the day. He reserved the front seat for us, as my walking was not at its best. We had a wonderful holiday and by the end of the week the courier and I were friends.

One day we came round a corner in the forest and straight in front of us was a big black bear. The driver had to put his brakes on quickly, and the bear just looked at us and walked back into the forest. We flew in a four-seater plane over the tops of the snow-covered mountains and could not believe that trees and waterfalls with numerous plants were growing on them.

We covered thousands of miles during the holiday. One day we had a picnic lunch on the beach and another day we pulled into a car park to get some food and a coffee and in the corner of the carpark were six massive lorries. I said to Marina, 'How would you like to sit in one of those?' I went up to the driver of a massive gleaming red truck and said we were on holiday from England, and we did not have lorries that size. I asked him if my partner could have her photo taken with him. He looked at Marina with a glint in his eye, and said 'sure, get in the cab.' It was about six feet from the ground, so the driver put up a step and helped her inside the cab. I took some lovely photos and he said, with a smile, 'Shall I drive off with Marina?' I said 'Not likely. Who would look after me?' He laughed and lowered her to the ground.

Canada is a beautiful and exciting place. The courier took our photos together and helped me on many occasions when I was walking badly. Marina was very happy, as she had always wanted to see the Rockies. We flew home and it felt very quiet to settle down to normal life.

Tristan, my gardener, had been looking after the garden while we were away. Fourteen acres is a lot to look after with twenty-five-foot polytunnels, but it was lovely to look down the garden. It was like being in a different world. I decided we should start to plant unusual trees and we planted two foxglove trees with their huge leaves. We also planted a pineapple tree with flowers that smelt like pineapple, and Marina bought me a tulip tree for my birthday. We also planted a yew tree and a redwood tree (the redwood will grow to 240 feet high). We already had a strawberry tree which is around eighteen feet high and has a lovely cream flower with small round 'strawberries'. The handkerchief tree we planted has white bracts that look like fluttering handkerchiefs.

We had opened the garden to charity because people who visited frequently asked why it hadn't been opened for others to enjoy. Anyone reading this book should visit the garden when coming to Cornwall, as it is different from any other garden.

We went over to the Isles of Scilly for a holiday and visited the famous Tresco gardens. We liked them so much we went back another two days. It was a lot of walking, but I managed it with my walking stick.

The following year we decided to visit Marina's sister Eleanor in Mandurah, Western Australia, and as it was a long journey I said to Eleanor that if she organised the holiday trips I would pay. I must say that Eleanor did a wonderful job with planes, hotels and shows all booked for us. We flew to Sydney to see the Opera House and I saw the famous bridge, which I wanted to climb. Marina and Eleanor stopped me as the temperature had risen to 42 degrees. I was very disappointed, but we had a lovely boat trip under the bridge.

We went to the Blue Mountains and saw the stone formations known as the Three Sisters. We then went on the steepest railway in the world. We had to be strapped in as it was a sheer vertical drop and our hair nearly took off!

Next morning we went by car to have breakfast overlooking the Blue Mountains. When we left the restaurant I spotted what looked like a racing car track. Marina and Eleanor said they were not going on that, but while they were not looking I booked a ticket. I got into a small racing car and it started to go faster and faster. I was holding this steering wheel for dear life when suddenly I was overtaken by a mother and daughter who waved to me and disappeared. On reaching the bottom they told me they were from Mauritius. To get back to the top I travelled in a cable car – what an experience!

We then flew to New Zealand, where a coach was waiting for us. We went to Christchurch and saw all the damage from the earthquake. They had erected a lot of modern buildings, including the church, which did not look in keeping with the original. Our coach took us on a road full of bends, with a sheer drop on one side and the sea on the other side. We stopped and went down to a cave. We could hear the roar of the stream which flowed down the middle of the cave and the roof was covered with thousands and thousands of glow worms. The boat rocked from side to side and we had to hold on for dear life. The whole experience was magical, but it was nice to see daylight again.

About eighteen months later, Eleanor invited us back to her home in Mandurah and arranged a further holiday trip to Sydney, Canberra and Melbourne. The coach turned into a derelict farm entrance, where we were met by the farmer and his wife and invited to sit down for a steak dinner. The steaks were about two inches thick and eight inches long. They were the best steaks we had ever tasted, and still are to this day. The farmer was doing the place up and had just bought two giant leaded windows. I told him about my experience in the glass business. He was quite impressed and showed me all around. We went to a number of vineyard 'tasters'. Then we went to a crayfish farm and saw thousands of crayfish being bred. We had a delicious crayfish meal with salad and potatoes. When we got to Canberra we went on a guided tour of Parliament House, where we sat in the chairs and heard Members of Parliament speaking.

We also caught the coach from Melbourne along the coast road and called in at a zoo called Maru Koala and Animal Park. Marina had her photo taken with a koala on her shoulder. We then came into a large grass area where we were greeted with a number of kangaroos, which came dashing towards us. We had light refreshments there, boarded the coach and headed towards Phillip Island, the home of fairy penguins. As it was still daylight, we had a meal in the complex. We then went to an area of seats placed in a semi-circular area very close to the beach. It was very cold and we had to wait until it was dark. We were straining our eyes to see the Fairy penguins when suddenly we saw a black mass rushing towards us from the sea. They all filtered to our right behind a fence and we rushed to the fence. There were hundreds of them, and the nearest were only about two feet from us. They were making their way to their burrows and took no notice of us. It was a very moving moment. Another wonderful and exciting trip to Australia.

I'm not going to bore you with all our other holidays, except to say that my grandson booked Marina and me on a four-week holiday in a five-star hotel in Costa Adeja, Tenerife. We had a lovely room with a balcony overlooking the swimming pool, and the food was excellent. It was not my scene really as I like adventure holidays, but I got to like it and ventured into the pool. A lot of the ladies did exercises in the water under an instructor. It was nice to watch, and I was hoping they would fall over in the water!

It was quite a way to walk from the hotel to the promenade. We stopped at a place that sold tours and booked up to go on a boat to watch dolphins. We found the boat and got on, but half way out I was seasick. The dolphins came right up to the boat. There was a crew of two with four passengers. We got back to the harbour and we were served with a hot meal. On the way back the wind blew my hat off and the last time I saw it it was floating on the sea. Probably some dolphin is now wearing it!

We were treated to an outdoor show with a three-course meal included plus three different bottles of wine. We toured the island of Tenerife in a coach. The road was cut through volcanic rock; very black. The hotel had entertainment every night and the waiter served us at our table. They did some lovely cocktails and suggested one called 'Sex on the Beach'. Marina and I thought they were great. We went to the local market and both bought several things but wow, my back was killing me. From the promenade we had to hire a taxi to take us back to the hotel. It was a lovely place, but if we went again we would want to stay closer to the promenade.

Although I had disliked cruises, I decided to book a cruise through Tui on a liner called *Marella Dream*. By this time my back was a lot worse, so I used my four-wheeled trolley. I thought we had booked

Marina and I

a cabin with double windows and balcony and we were shown into a cabin with one porthole; we were very disappointed.

To get to the restaurant for breakfast it was a quarter-mile walk. The food was very nice and there were tables reserved for the disabled. A small swimming pool was outside the restaurant and we tried to sit down on the lounge chairs provided, but it was too cold and windy. I was not at all well and had a stomach upset; not nice. We played bingo in the afternoon. To walk round the boat was about a mile and I could only do half.

We then booked a coach tour and went to see performing dolphins at Rancho Park Texas in Lanzarote. They had five of them dancing. The gangway was very steep and my trolley had to be carried up to the top by one of the crew. I think Marina liked it and the waiter took a liking to her, but I was pleased to get home.

I then booked a safari holiday to Kenya, but had to cancel due to going into hospital, which was very disappointing. I wanted to show Marina all the wildlife in the bush. We visited several more open gardens and then Covid 19 descended upon us, and we had to cancel the garden openings for a while. Hopefully we will resume in 2022.

During the last few years we had been to Chelsea Flower Show twice and Hampton Court Flower Show (which is where we met). I was having difficulty walking now and was not sure if I could do this again.

I had a surprise for my birthday. Vanessa, Marina's daughter, had booked us into a hotel at Malvern to see a flower show at Malvern Three Counties showground. We had an afternoon tea at Stow-on-the-Wold on the way up. The next morning we parked in the showground car park and I thought I would not be able to walk around the show with my walking stick, but Vanessa had hired me a mobile scooter to get around. It was a lovely show and we saw marrows over one hundredweight each, parsnips that were three feet long and a wonderful show of flowers, including a children's section. We queued up to get fish and chips and the weather was so cold that the chips nearly walked off the plate. Vanessa looked frozen. The scooter had been a godsend, and I was able to see the whole show before we headed home.

Marina was very keen on fuchsias, so we joined the Fowey Fuchsia Club. When the annual show came around we could not compete with the quality of the exhibits, but we did win three prizes.

We had been with the club about three years and learned at the annual meeting that they wanted a new chairman. Nobody volunteered, and all eyes were on me. I said 'Whoa, I'm in my eighties!' They kept looking at me and I weakened, and somebody said 'I propose Derek Bishop for Chairman; All those in favour?' Every member of the club put their hand up and that was that.

Marina, who is on the committee now, helps me a great deal and we help in preparing the school hall for the shows. I now have to open the show, hand out the cups to the prize winners, thank the judge and thank everyone for coming. Members are invited to see the bluebell woods, and committee meetings are held at my house. Marina and I now manage to win several prizes and sometimes I have to present a cup to myself!

John Sweet, a friend of mine, took us out one Sunday to a garden called Trebah near Falmouth. What a garden! I consider it one of the finest in Cornwall. It has a magnificent collection of ferns (some fourteen feet high), and a magnificent collection of rhododendrons and camellias. It has a huge natural lake full of fish and a Monet-style bridge to cross down at the end of the garden. There is a long stone wall with a small door within it. On opening the door you go down steep steps and in front of you is a beach with cliffs and rocks on both sides. There was a small stone building on the beach and we bought an ice cream each and sat on the wall in the blazing sun. We read a sign on the wall that described how the Americans had used the beach to train during World War Two and it showed landing craft full of troops, practising how to land when invading. Trebah had built a lovely restaurant where you can get a great lunch, reasonably-priced.

We have both joined as members and enjoy going around the gardens, which have given me a lot of ideas for my own garden.

Marina and I are now a couple, and I am glad I have met somebody so caring. We have shared some lovely trips. One day I saw an advert in the paper for a trip to a concert by Andre Rieu in Maastricht. When we arrived there, we stayed in a nice hotel and enjoyed an excellent evening meal. We were very tired and went off to bed.

The next day we got on a coach and toured the countryside. All the fields were level and had dykes on each side to contain the water from flooding. We also saw an original windmill in working order. After lunch we arrived for the concert about 6.30pm. There were people everywhere, all the restaurants were full and the whole of the forecourts were full of excited people waiting for the arrival of Andre Rieu. We had lovely seats with an eight-foot walkway in front of us. Suddenly a roar went up and Andre, with his entire cast, came walking by us waving and smiling at all of us. He came within three feet of us. The excitement of the people was magical.

They took their places on the stage and Andre welcomed us to his concert; 8,000 people in the open air. The music was wonderful and the band was superb. Andre said everyone needed music in their life, and we had famous singers and dancers. The lady who played the piano took off her outer dress and tap danced on top of the piano.

The highlight of the evening was when 150 dancers from all the dancing schools joined the Viennese waltz two at a time and danced right in front of us, then glided down the aisles. They were superbly dressed in white and there were about 12 groups of disabled dancers in wheelchairs. It brought tears to my eyes. Andre could certainly play the violin; we were mesmerised.

Near the end of the show there was a fantastic firework display and the sky was lit up in different colours. The crowd called for more. Andre said there would be no more and then started to pack up. We all stood up and shouted for more, and he said it was his bed time. 'Do we still want more?' he said. 'Yes!' we all shouted, 'More!

more! more!' He then said 'Are you sure?' It was deafening, with the audience shouting 'YES!'

The whole band joined in and all the singers. One musician had a pint of beer and was spilling it as he drank, pretending he was drunk. He passed the glass to the other musicians.

It was nearly 12.15 when Andre led the company off the stage, all passing in front of us and continuing right through the crowds, waving and laughing. What a man! What an evening! Everyone was clapping and shouting. We got back to our hotel at about 12.45.

I have a confession to make; before we saw the advert in the paper I had never heard of Andre Rieu. We are now both hooked on his style of music.

After that Andre came to England and we booked a coach to see the show in Birmingham. It lacked the power of Maastricht, but was a wonderful show. Later in the year the Maastricht show was put on at our local cinema in Wadebridge. Every time the local cinema shows Andre we are there. I have always been busy with some project and have never had much time for music, but seeing these shows has changed my perception on life. Marina also likes Irish country music and I have been converted. During the week we turn the TV over at 10 o'clock to watch. I even know some of the words to the music. I tap my feet and thoroughly enjoy it. Many thanks to Andre Rieu for converting me to music; everyone needs music, although I cannot understand the modern songs of today.

At the age of 86 years I suddenly thought it would be nice to go to America and see the Grand Canyon. I suggested it to Marina, and she said she would love to go, and although my walking was deteriorating I booked the tickets to America. We caught a plane from Heathrow and landed in San Francisco on 17th September 2016. The hotel was lovely and we booked several excursions during the trip.

Looking forward to boarding the coach the next morning we got up, had breakfast and went to meet the coach. At reception we found it had departed without us and another couple as well. I was furious, and although the reception was sympathetic I said to Marina that we would have to entertain ourselves. We went outside the hotel and in front of us was one of the famous trams. We got on with our feet dangling, it took our breath away and we thought it was a good start. When we got out at the end we found ourselves in a small market, and I bought a lovely pen with a polished wood stem. I use this pen every day and when I am writing I think of the time I bought it.

We then strolled into the main market, saw an information desk and explained what had happened, and the receptionist said she would make a list of places to visit. We bought two tickets to go on a boat trip and had a crab salad for lunch on a seat overlooking the harbour. The boat went by Alcatraz, the famous prison, and under the famous Golden Gate bridge. The size of the bridge made us gasp.

Back on dry land, we got on an open-top bus which went over the bridge. It was very cold and we shivered all the way. We then caught the tram, this time going up a steep slope. When we got back at about 6.30pm, I went to see the courier and before she could utter a word I gave her a good telling off. When she was able to get a word in she explained that our names were not on the list. I forgave her and the rest of the coach conceded that our day had been more rewarding and exciting. Mary, the courier, was able to get on to her office and get our money back.

When we all got on the coach the next day, the courier was laughing as she asked if everyone was on board. We stayed at a place called Furnace Creek where there was a small museum showing all the different rocks and stones; I bought a piece of fool's gold. In the evening we decided to go and see a local show called Fat Trap and enjoyed a meal. The place looked full, but we were escorted to the front and shared a table with some Americans who were fascinated by the way that Marina spoke (she was born in Cornwall). We had a lovely evening, but when we went outside it was snowing a blizzard. We were standing there, very cold, when a caravanette pulled up and the driver invited us to jump in – they took us right back to the ranch where we were staying. They were such nice people and they would not take any money.

The next morning we woke up to find everywhere covered in snow, although we had arrived the day before in brilliant sunshine. We proceeded to a place called Bryce Canyon, which was a breath-taking deep valley canyon of an orange rusty colour with a steep twisted path snaking down to the bottom. I could not walk down, but we stood on the roots of a large tree watching people going down, looking smaller and smaller. It was an amazing sight. A mist came in, changing all the colours of the rocks and pinnacles to red, yellow and orange. Marina and I did not want to leave, but the coach driver was calling us.

We travelled through miles and miles of barren scenery with cactus trees 15-20 feet high rising from the landscape. Back at the hotel, we and had a cowboy meal with entertainment. Next day, after a lovely breakfast, we travelled to Monument Valley, which is a tow-ering formation with red rocks in many different shapes. We got off the coach and were driven down a steep bumpy track to reach the bottom. Lots of Western films were made in Monument Valley with the likes of John Wayne and the director John Ford.

We stood at one large rock and looked up through a large hole in the rock. I started talking to three or four of our party about part of my life and my garden, and suddenly about twenty-five people were listening. When I finished they all clapped me and thanked me for a most entertaining talk. Marina said it sounded good and I had come up in the world.

Next day the coach took us to the Grand Canyon in brilliant sun-shine. We queued up to get on one of the helicopters. Suddenly we were in the air – the first time either of us had been in a helicopter. We flew down between the canyon walls and far below us the Colorado River was flowing; a wonderful sight, and we took lots of photos.

Next day, back on the coach, we travelled about a hundred miles. We came to a flat area at the top of a steep incline and stopped at an

Indian market. Looking around, I saw a horse standing on top of a large rock area looking over the valley. Our courier, Mary Klepper, took us to see the horse, a mustang stallion, and asked if anybody would like to volunteer to get on it. No one stepped forward and I said to Marina, 'Shall we?' Her answer was yes, so I stepped forward to get on. It had been trained in the last twelve months. A man dressed as a cowboy gave me a hat and with help I got one leg over and was stuck. Mary and the cowboy, with Marina's help, finally got me on the horse. I felt I had been split in two! I then sat upright and waved my hat at the crowd, who were watching from the coach. They all clapped and laughed.

Now came the problem of how I was going to get off. The three of them tried to get me down without success. I was sweating now and stuck, and I thought I was going to fall off. I gripped the horse, digging my fingers into his body, and he never flinched. I finally got off and bowed to the crowd and they were congratulating me. I said 'I'm not bad for an 85-year-old with a bad back!'

Marina then got on the horse, with a little trouble, and the cowboy helped us off. I am quite famous on the holiday tours as the man on the horse, and the courier, Mary, has put the photo on Facebook. She still keeps in contact.

We made a short journey back to Palm Springs, California, and were able to see the homes of the film stars. We went on the world's longest revolving cable car, then had a walk round the shops and found one called Ooh-La-La. We had a laugh and went in. I bought some swimming trunks and Marina bought a swimming costume, as the hotel we were staying at had a swimming pool.

That evening we went for a meal at an Italian restaurant and they had a singer and suddenly she came up and sat on my lap. She sung 'Happy birthday Derek,' and everybody clapped - then they brought a small birthday cake with one candle. Marina had arranged it. A lovely surprise, Marina is such a loving and supportive partner.

Next day we were off to Hollywood; what a place! It was so busy.

We saw the Hollywood sign and then visited the famous Hollywood Walk of Fame.

This was the last day of the holiday. We drove back to Los Angeles Airport and overnight we flew home to the UK. It was a wonderful holiday and we were very grateful to our driver, our courier and New Market Holidays.

CHAPTER 12

# Looking back

When I first moved to Cornwall, I started a company called Kean Estates (industrial Holdings) Ltd with the trademark 'Karen Homes'. As I am writing this today the company has been trading for over 50 years and has built over 400 homes. When I came to Cornwall, I bought over £250,000 of land and then went to the bank to finance these purchases. At one time the company had nearly half a million pounds in overdraft. We have survived two recessions when we nearly went under, but were supported by the bank. When building some estates, I never built the same design on any two sites. I have enjoyed the excitement of building houses and bungalows and seeing the joy in people when handing the keys over for their new property. Today I am still in contact with some of the property clients and enjoy seeing them and have lunch together.

The secret of the first success has been that all the land we bought is still valued in the accounts at the purchase price and people are not aware of its true value. We have received several offers to buy the company but have not succumbed. I have run this company without seeking favours from anyone, and this has caused me a lot of problems from the planning officers in Cornwall. They continually blocked my planning applications, and in the end I was forced to stop building. The company kept the land, and Sheila and I took no salary or dividends from the company. We continued to plug away and obtained planning on land. We felt we had been unfairly treated. As I described earlier, we bought a piece of land at Seaton in Cornwall with planning permission for eighteen bungalows, but a year later we forgot to renew the planning, so the Council would not renew. So we had a piece of land worth nothing after several years of trying for planning and being refused.

We did not give up and as I alluded to earlier, I was approached by a friend, who said he knew somebody who dealt with difficult planning proposals. This consultant said he could not help me but he knew somebody called Nigel Cant who might be able to help. This proved to be very expensive, but it produced results. Nigel, a man in his 60s, studied all the documents and said he would undertake the proposal, but it would cost several thousand pounds. He did a lot of research and thought that permission dated 1960 was still viable. He submitted a planning application, which was refused, and we lodged an appeal. It took several months for the appeal to take place and the inspector ruled in our favour, the planning was still in play, and the inspector awarded all our costs (£18,000) to Cornwall Council. The council were livid and decided to appeal, but the Inspector said they would lose and would have to pay us substantial damages. The council backed off, but this was just the start of a vicious campaign against the company.

However I believe that persistence pays off. I had been going to courses on carving figures in Portland stone and the people who ran the courses lived in a contemporary bungalow built on stilts, with a lot of floor-to-ceiling windows and open-plan living areas. It was their building that prompted his wife to suggest I should approach their architects, Arco2 from Bodmin. Arco2 were award-winning architects and after meeting them, I engaged them to plan twelve houses in the most modern design that has ever been drawn; they were breathtaking. Plans were submitted and then came the opposition; too modern, not in keeping, too dense, too high in elevation, basically everything the opposition could throw at it.

The architects pursued it and a compromise was agreed; ten houses instead of twelve, two storeys instead of three. We put in a new drainage system and tarmac with no expense to the house holders. I engaged a contractor to tarmac the road and drainage system and put in all the services to the houses. I had spent £300,000 and decided to sell the site. It was valued at over one million pounds. After many ups and downs, I have finally had an offer for £950,000 which we have accepted, but we are still waiting for the contract to be signed as the contract has now been issued. As I have always said, it is not sold until the money is in the bank. I must thank the planner for not letting me build because the return of £950,000 is not a bad return on a purchase of £18,000.

I had another site in Downderry in Cornwall with the same circumstances, but the Council decided not to refuse planning this time. We purchased this site for £9,500 in 1973 and sold off bits and pieces for £12,000, and the land has just been sold and gone to contract for £750,000 with only £25,000 in expenses, so not a bad return. The company has still got other sites we cannot sell due to the amount of tax we have got to pay. I have appointed my grandson as a director of the company and he said he would like to keep the company going for a long time after I have passed on.

The company account has been handwritten for fifty years but my grandson wishes to computerise. I have said that when we have an accounts system that is suitable, I shall be surplus to requirements as I do not have a computer and have no compulsion to get one!

Marina and I are keen gardeners, and with Tristan and Karen, we have been able to open up the 14 acres of gardens for charity three times a year. As I have previously outlined, when I built Fontana, there was no garden. It was all brambles, bracken and fallen trees. I owned a digging machine and two men and I went down through the

brambles and cut a track through the undergrowth. We then decided to have a huge bonfire which cleared the site bare. I do not work with drawings. I looked at the top of the site and thought I would build an Italian garden. I imported a fountain and statues from Italy. The digger driver carved a round section in the top of the site and then we built a circular retaining wall using all the granite rocks picked up in the garden. We installed the fountain in the centre and paved all round it with patterned bricks in four colours. We had to put a series of steps to get down to it and another series of steps to get down to part of the garden behind the circular wall.

I planted a handkerchief tree which was then about six feet high and today, in 2021, it is about 35 feet high with about 150 little 'handkerchiefs' fluttering. The garden is quite steep with one side at about a 45-degree angle. We cut a track through the middle as the surrounding trees were about 110 years old and mostly rotten, dangerous and falling over. We got out a chainsaw, cut them down and cut them into logs to give away. We did have that visit from the Tree Preservation Officer, as some nosey busybody had reported us. He was very courteous and he advised that in the future we should ring him when we were considering cutting down any trees. He commented on what a lovely job we were making of the garden.

We now had a magnificent view over the countryside. After reshaping the hillside, I bought some trees and five tree ferns. We had inherited a large pond which was overgrown with brambles and you could not walk around it because of a steep slope. We had a stream running through the middle of the garden and in front of that about an acre of ground. If you stood in this area your feet would be sucked in. We installed a number of drainage pipes and tracked in all surplus soil,

then made the area up by about ten feet and created a path around the pond.

I had now bought a Kubota tractor with a trailer, and I was using it going up the new track and was nearly at the top when it toppled over and I was trapped underneath. I wriggled my legs and arms and was able to move them. Then I managed to wriggle out from under the tractor. I had a lucky escape due to the safety arm which stopped the tractor from toppling down the slope. I shall be more careful in the future.

We planted a lot of new plants and trees, including a foxglove tree, fire bush tree, eucalyptus, magnolias, rhododendrons and camellia bushes. This part of this garden was shaping up and the other side of the garden was an acer glade planted in 1956 by the railway homes, and underneath was about two and a half acres of bluebells. What a sight when they are out; one blue haze with snowdrops and wild hyacinths popping up in between times. We still have a lot of bracken coming up, and when the bluebells have finished blooming we strim the whole area.

One of the first flowers out in spring are the primroses. We have about 250,000. It gives you a good feeling when walking through. I often give friends a couple of primroses to take home as a present from Fontana. At the bottom of the garden was about two acres of forest with a lot of trees over 100 years old. The problem was that there was no access, so we bulldozed a winding track through the forest. On one side we exposed a wall made of stone standing about nine feet high. I thought how naked it all looked, but after three years you would never have guessed it had been done. We keep the forest natural and any trees that fall down are left just where they fell.

After five years the garden was beginning to look like something; two of the tree ferns we had planted earlier were growing well but three looked sad. We found out we needed to plant them closer to water, so we dug the holes out and got the machine in to dig under them and carry them to the new site. Today we have 18 tree ferns, some of which are eight feet high. The rule is if that if they are looking sick, we dig them up and replant in another piece of the garden.

We had some Chusan palms about 30 feet high and planted six banana trees surrounded by bamboo. We built a 70-foot high waterfall and dug out a large pond, installing a bore hole pump to pump the water up the hill. I wanted to have a polytunnel, but pondered where to place it without spoiling the look of the garden. I looked around and spied a sloping piece of garden close to the house. We needed a machine to get to it, but the path in front of the conservatory was only three feet wide. We located and hired this machine, which could be pulled in with just two inches to spare. We were able to dig a flat piece of ground forty feet long by fourteen feet wide, which was enough to place a polytunnel of thirty feet by twelve feet. We were able to grow a lot of the plants we wanted and grew our own tomatoes and cucumbers. It soon became full, so we had the machine in once again and managed to get another piece of ground for another tunnel twenty five feet by twelve feet with about one foot left before a slope about nine feet high.

All this was made from a piece of land carved out of a hillside. I planted a lot more trees including a London plane tree, oak trees, fig trees, bean tree, pittisporum and maple. We now open the garden for charity and I take visitors down the garden, but if someone asks me the name of that tree or bush and I can't remember I make up a name and carry on. Up to now I have never been queried!

Over time this has made several thousand pounds for the Hospice. I am only an amateur gardener and find most gardening is common sense. This year we decided to see how many types of trees are in the garden; we were shocked to see that we have at least 46 varieties. I do hope when anyone reading this book visits Cornwall, they will visit the garden with their friends. I am sure you will enjoy it.

I am experiencing a problem getting around my garden. The years are going by, my back is playing me up and I paid to see a consultant who told me my back is worn out. At my age they cannot do anything for me, and much to my disgust, I have to use a four-wheel frame to get around outside. I have bought a golf trolley, which Marina found on the internet.

Tristan, my gardener, is now employed full time and is a great help to me. As I write this in 2021 I have not been down the garden for six months due to the virus which is sweeping the world. We must now wear masks and keep six feet apart. Garden visits are not possible at the moment and we are praying for a cure to overcome this dreadful disease.

In 2019 we got a new Prime Minister. Boris Johnson was voted to power to take us out of Europe in what is called 'Brexit'. I personally think it is a good idea not to be ruled by Europe. Boris had been in power for about three months when suddenly the whole world was in the grip of Covid 19. The pandemic originated in China, but soon millions of people around the world were contracting it and thousands were dying from it. Old people and old people's homes were considered the worst risk, and my family agreed with Marina that I should isolate and stay with her in Wadebridge. The whole world was turned upside down and we were told to wear masks when going out, not to mix with other households. When in shops and elsewhere we are to be two metres apart and not to make any unnecessary car journeys. I had booked my 89th birthday party at Trenython Manor, which is now a luxury hotel, but had to cancel.

In 2021 things have started to get better; fewer people are dying and going into hospital. The country has been placed into four tier groups of restrictions and Cornwall was placed in Tier 1. In London and other high tier areas, shops were closed. Pubs, restaurants and many companies were suffering. The Government had to subsidise the workers, so they brought in a scheme called furlough, which paid 80 percent of their wages. The country is now many billions of pounds in debt.

Then suddenly a new strain of the virus appeared which was much worse and spread more quickly. A number of the population would not stick to the rules, which was very selfish of them. Then our Prime Minister was criticised by some for doing too much and by others for not doing enough; he was in a no-win situation. The new virus has taken grip of the whole country and everyday there are more cases and deaths. Cornwall is in lockdown, but suddenly the cases have more than doubled, and people keep coming down to Cornwall on holiday and bringing the virus with them. They are now being turned back and told to go home.

Boris Johnson then put the whole of the country in full lockdown. If only people would stick to the rules. There has also been some good news with vaccines being produced, and I had a telephone call to summon me to Bodmin Hospital for an injection. It was very well organised and we had a restful 15 minutes afterwards. I found I was sitting next to a lady of 100 years of age and said to her, 'how well you walk. I'm 89 and I can't walk far'. She smiled and said, 'you're still a baby yet, lift up your legs and walk'.

Marina and I have been toying with the idea of getting married and are still discussing at the moment. I am in quarantine and I am so well looked after; it will be hard to go home when this virus is over. I am now in my 90th year.

My grandson Robert has just announced that he and his girlfriend are going to get married in 2022. My business is prospering, so I pray that I can have a few more years. I have had a wonderful life, and a loving wife in Sheila, to whom I was married for 54 years. My daughter Karen who has helped me through, and especially my partner Marina, who has now been with me for eight years.

It has been a revelation writing this book. I hope you have enjoyed it and that you will visit my garden at Fontana. With God's help, I may see you when you visit.

Derek Bishop
April 2021